Sports Illustrated

PETER KING

MONDAY MORNING QUARTERBACK

Sports Illustrated

PETER KING

MONDAY MORNING QUARTERBACK

A fully caffeinated guide to everything
you need to know about the NFL

Edited by LARRY BURKE

To my wonderful wife Ann, the smart one,
who never wanted to be in the column.

To my daughters Laura and Mary Beth,
who thought it was cool to be in the column.

And to Mike McGuire, who, I hope, showed America through
the column what a valiant profession soldiering is—
and who taught me, one of the biggest doves on the planet,
how important soldiering is.

ICON KEY

Things I Think
I Think

Factoids That May
Interest Only Me

They Said It

Stats

Money

Movies

TV

Music

Predictions:
I'm a Genius

Predictions:
I'm an Idiot

Contents

Introduction... 8

MMQB Classic: *Three-Quarterback Monte*........... 13

MMQB Classic: *A Rather Good Color Man* 20

Ten Things I Think I Think: *Commish for a Day*..... 25

MMQB Classic: *Why Peyton Manning is MVP*...... 33

MMQB Classic: *A Matter of Perspective* 44

Ten Things I Think I Think: *Top Coaching Hires* 50

MMQB Classic: *Terrell Davis's Mystery Injury*....... 53

MMQB Classic: *Helping a Giant Cause*.............. 57

Greats of the Game: *My Top 100 Players of Today*...... 66

MMQB Classic: *The Sincerest Form of Flattery*...... 77

MMQB Classic: *Field Hockey Novella* 83

Ten Things I Think I Think: *Best Draft Picks*........ 91

MMQB Classic: *Chris Canty's Free-Agency Foray*... 94

MMQB Classic: *Foul Ball*........................... 102

Ten Things I Think I Think: *Hall of Fame Snubs*... 109

ICON KEY

Planes

Trains

Automobiles

MMQB Classic: *Family Matters* 114

MMQB Classic: *A Field Trip Like No Other* 119

Ten Things I Think I Think: *SI Covers* ...... photo insert

MMQB Classic: *Score Another Patriots Victory* 129

MMQB Classic: *Goodbye, Woody* 135

Ten Things I Think I Think: *Clichés I Hate* 143

MMQB Classic: *John Elway Rides Off* 147

MMQB Classic: *Christmas Presence* 150

Greats of the Game: *My Top 100 Players of All Time* ... 158

MMQB Classic: *On the Range with Brett Favre* 169

MMQB Classic: *Prep Squad* 177

Ten Things I Think I Think: *NFL's Best, Worst* 188

MMQB Classic: *Chemistry with Mike Martz* 197

MMQB Classic: *Tears and Then Cheers* 202

Peter King's Football America: *Map Quest* 210

Acknowledgments 255

Hotels

Airports

Coffeenerdness

Baseball

From the Notebook

From the Mailbag

From the Tabloids

Introduction

A FEW THINGS HAVE shocked me in my life. The Red Sox winning the pennant in 1967. SPORTS ILLUSTRATED wanting to hire me in 1989. A woman who has liked me enough to stay married to me for 30 years. But a conversation I had with my SI.com editor, Dom Bonvissuto, after the 2010 NFL draft is right up there. I asked Dom about how our business was going, and our business, the web business, is all about page views. "Well, your postdraft MMQB generated 2.9 million page views," he said. Hmmm. That means almost the same number of people clicked onto my column on a Monday in April as subscribe to SI. And as we publish the paperback version of the MMQB book we put out last fall, that's as good a place to start as any. How'd we ever get to this point?

I N THE FALL OF 1997, print journalism still seemed as solid as a rock. Beat guys for big newspapers were starting to make six-figure salaries, and top columnists had long since reached that threshold. But none of us had any idea where the journalism business was going. There was this newfangled thing called the Internet, and newspapers and magazines were launching websites, having no idea if it was a passing fad or the way of the future. At SPORTS ILLUSTRATED, my former pro football editor, Steve Robinson, had been tapped to run SI's new 24-hour sports cable TV channel, CNN/SI, and its companion sports website, CNNSI.com (soon to be renamed SI.com).

I liked Steve. I trusted him. One day he called me with a pitch for the new website. "This thing has to have original content from SI writers, and you have a voice in pro football that we'd like to tap," he said.

At the time, I was the pro football insider on a Sunday morning CNN NFL pregame show, and I attended a big NFL game each Sunday, writing the INSIDE THE NFL column for the magazine each week. It was a fairly full plate that Steve wanted to make fuller. But what he had in mind struck a chord with me. I remember Steve's saying that day, "You're an old newspaper guy. You've got stuff in your notebook that you probably just throw away at the end of the week. What if you took that stuff, plus stuff from Sunday's games, and you wrote a column for Monday morning?" Put some strong opinions in there, he said, and if you had dinner with someone Saturday night you wanted to talk about, feel free.

Two thoughts hit me. One: *Oh boy! More work!* Two: *Nobody at the magazine seems all fired up to work for this Internet thing, so why should I be?* But I figured it wouldn't take that long, and what was 600 or 800 more words to write?

You know the rest of the story. Eight hundred words a week has become 8,000. And because the NFL off-season has essentially been eliminated, I now write Monday Morning Quarterback 48 weeks a year instead of 24.

For better or worse, you learned far too much about Brett Favre on and off the field, Laura and Mary Beth King on softball and field hockey fields, Mike McGuire on the fields of war. You met my dogs; you went into the vet's office to share the compassionate death of Woody. You learned that I like my coffee strong, I hate hotels that charge to use the gym, I love Amtrak, I don't like Terrell Owens, I like most everything about New Jersey, I don't like kids who take foul balls that don't belong to them and I love the smell of the grass in the morning in Latrobe, Pa. And you learned about a few other things, like traveling colonoscopy preparation. (That's one that I'd like to have back, by the way.)

The column has morphed into something like 78% football, 22% personal stuff and opinions. I've been relatively unfiltered. The only time I've been asked to not write about something was Dom Bonvissuto's plea to keep politics out of MMQB in the last couple of years. In other words, keep my left-of-center leanings to myself. A good plan, based on the e-mails I got from the far right of Rush Limbaugh when I did venture into a political opinion.

It has become a nice pastime for me, writing anything I want; and you've become a great core of readers. So the editor of SI, Terry McDonell, asked me to write a Monday Morning Quarterback book. I'm sure he had either a National Book Award or the bottom line in mind; had to be one of those. And that's how this project was born.

S O ALONG WITH THANKING Terry—and the loyal readers of Monday Morning Quarterback on SI.com—for making this book a reality, I have to thank Steve Robinson.

"I don't want to be like Al Gore when he said he invented the Internet," Steve said. He's semiretired now, living in Florida with his family. "But I'm happy that I helped create a franchise that has thrived. There were people at the magazine who thought we were letting you get away with too much—personal stuff, mostly—and that maybe you'd gone too far afield. But it was you conversing with your readers about Mary Beth and softball and coffee and hotels on the road, and I thought we should just roll with it. The real idea of the column was to get a lot of behind-the-scenes football, dinner with quarterbacks, talking to coaches in lobbies. You became a lot of readers' window into the NFL. And writing on the Web became writing with more personality, and most readers liked that."

"But," I said, "there had to be something you didn't like—some time you wanted to tell me, 'Peter, enough.'"

"Well," Steve said, "The stories about Mary Beth and softball tested some people's patience."

Everybody's got an opinion. That's why we invented the Tuesday version of MMQB, to let you tell me I'm an idiot for bragging about my kids.

I hope that's one of the reasons why you click—that you can read me, tell me I'm all wet and I'll listen.

AND I HOPE that's why this book will work. It's a collection of the columns I've liked the most and tidbits I've liked the most over the years. There's some new stuff not from MMQB, and a bunch of things I did just because it's my book. This is the new and (I hope) improved paperback version. I went back and updated a few things. For instance, I massacred my ranking of the top 100 players of today, moving the likes of Darrelle Revis way up and dropping Albert Haynesworth way down. Most other things I kept intact.

As always, you can send me your thoughts. Sound off to me at SI.com (peter_king@simail.com) or on Twitter (SI_PeterKing). I'll be reading, and responding to, your comments. I think I think that's why we've become a good team, you and me.

MMQB Classic April 26, 2004

Three- Quarterback Monte

Giants G.M. Ernie Accorsi was the man in the middle of a high-stakes draft game that paid off all around

Draft weekend, 2004. I had someone in San Diego who was telling me, daily, not to give up on a Giants-Chargers megadeal that would enable San Diego to get draft choices as well as Philip Rivers, and the Giants to get Eli Manning—even though the Giants and Chargers kept saying that wouldn't happen. I've always loved reconstructing big stories, and this quarterback deal that would direct the fortunes of three teams is one of my alltime favorites.

One of the strangest things in NFL draft history happened on Saturday afternoon around 12:45 in East Rutherford, N.J. I'm not sure that even everyone in the New York Giants draft room knows exactly what occurred to make this possible.

Within a span of about eight minutes, Giants G.M. Ernie Accorsi had his tentacles into all

What do Bill Parcells and Hank Aaron have in common? Both homered off Al Downing; Parcells as a youth in New Jersey American Legion ball and Aaron in a ball game slightly more important.

13

Landing in Harrisburg one morning at the inaptly named hut called Harrisburg International Airport, I heard this over the main P.A. system: "Your attention, please. Will the person who left the Certs at the security checkpoint please return to claim them immediately. Attention, please. Will the person who left the Certs at the security checkpoint please return to claim them immediately."

three of the marquee quarterbacks in this draft.

He quite literally had the fate of each one—Mississippi's Eli Manning, North Carolina State's Philip Rivers and Miami of Ohio's Ben Roethlisberger—in his hands midway through the 15-minute period that the Giants had to make the fourth overall choice on Saturday.

Now the story can be told. Accorsi, with 10 minutes left in the period, had an offer he liked on the table with Cleveland to trade the Giants' first-round pick down three spots to the Browns, in exchange for the Browns' seventh overall choice, plus Cleveland's second-rounder. With that pick, the Giants would take Roethlisberger, the cannon-armed passer whose right wing could cut through the overly brisk late-autumn winds at the Meadowlands. Then, with about eight minutes left in the Giants' period, San Diego general manager A.J. Smith called, trying to get the Giants to up their offer for Manning, who'd already been picked by San Diego. Accorsi was very interested. Before the deal could have all the i's dotted and t's crossed, the period would have expired, and so Accorsi had to pick Rivers. He had a verbal deal, and he was pretty sure it would get done, but you never know how these things might turn out. Then the correct paperwork was filed with the league, and the trade got done.

The Giants went from a solid deal that would have left them with Roethlisberger, to drafting Rivers, to trading for Manning—all in about half the time it takes to watch a *Seinfeld* rerun.

"You know," Accorsi said last night, "it all happened so fast that I didn't realize it at the time. But you're right. It's amazing. It's one of those things you'll remember for a long time."

To tell this tale, let's go back to the night before the draft. Accorsi got two interesting phone calls on Friday night. One, from the Chargers' Smith, was about San Diego's latest proposal to try to get this deal done. To this point, the Giants' best offer to acquire San Diego's top pick was their first- and third-rounds picks this year and their second next year. They modeled this deal after the Chargers' trade of the pick that ended up being Michael Vick to Atlanta three years ago. The only thing missing was a player; Atlanta had traded middling wideout Tim Dwight to San Diego as part of the 2001 Vick haul. The Giants were willing to give an O.K. player, but the Chargers were asking for defensive end Osi Umenyiora.

Who is Umenyiora, you ask? He's a second-round pick last year, from Troy State in Alabama, with good pass-rush potential. So now Smith asked Accorsi for their first-, second- and third-round picks this year, their first next year and

Pittsburgh back Jerome Bettis's rushing line against Oakland on Sept. 12, 2004, in a 24–21 win for the Steelers: Five carries, one yard, three TDs. That's seven inches per carry.

Umenyiora. It's not even close, Accorsi told him. The second call came from an Accorsi acquaintance, someone Accorsi felt was reliable, who told him the Chargers were planning to draft Manning and then try to trade him to the Giants in a package for Rivers as the first round progressed. Surprised at the revelation, Accorsi began thinking that he might have to act quickly if indeed that's the way the deal would transpire.

But he went to bed on Friday night thinking there was no way the bridge would be built, no way the Chargers would adjust their offer enough to get a deal done. And as the time ticked away on Saturday morning and Smith didn't call back, Accorsi just assumed that either the deal was dead or the Chargers maybe would call after the Manning pick. The draft began. San Diego picked Manning. No phone call. The Giants were up.

The phone rang. It was Cleveland's capologist, Lal Heneghan. The Browns, who had called two weeks before the draft wanting to move to the Giants' spot, confirmed that they would still give the Giants their first- and second-round picks in exchange for New York's top pick. The Giants would have to think about it. Accorsi was tempted, really tempted, but he worried that maybe Cleveland might then use the fourth pick to deal to San Diego to get either Manning or tackle Robert

"Tell Dan he's safe. Four years ... no way I'll be around that long."

—Brett Favre, following the 2002 season, when he was 106 touchdown passes behind Dan Marino's alltime record of 420. As we know now, he smashed Marino's record five years later.

Gallery. And if that happened, Oakland, at two, would simply take the guy the first team didn't take—Manning or Gallery.

Roethlisberger was looking mighty appealing, and that other pick from Cleveland, the 37th overall, might be a nice way to buttress a weak offensive line—say, with center Jake Grove from Virginia Tech.

Tick, tick, tick.

Less than eight minutes to go. Phone rang. It was Smith. "You haven't called," the Chargers G.M. said. "You still interested?" Accorsi was, and they started dueling over the phone. ("We were both playing poker," Accorsi said later.) For the Giants, including this year's second-rounder was out; they simply had to bolster that offensive line with a highly rated player. For the Chargers, the Giants had to include next year's first-round pick.

Four minutes. Three minutes.

"I knew we had one more play to make," Accorsi said last night. "I was holding back next year's one as the trump card." And now it came out: the one and three this year and the one next year. But Smith still wanted Umenyiora. A deal-breaker, Accorsi said. Smith said he had to have something. Accorsi offered a six in next year's draft. Smith wanted a four. They met in the middle. A five.

With the clock almost expired, the Giants had

From 11-10-08:
I think the Cleveland coaches are dead men walking.

The entire Browns staff was released at the end of its 4–12 season.

Back in the fall of 2000 the Center City Starbucks in Philadelphia charged 65 cents for a sesame bagel and 75 cents for a plain bagel. A sesame bagel is a plain bagel with sesame seeds added. That would mean, logically, that 100 sesame seeds cost minus 10 cents.

to take a leap of faith. The deal was done, but it hadn't been turned in to the league office. So they picked Rivers. When the ESPN cameras flashed to Rivers, he had the look of a 12-year-old watching *Texas Chainsaw Massacre*. The Giants didn't even call Rivers, sitting at home in North Carolina, to say the fix was in. A few minutes later, when the deal was official, the league announced it. Roethlisberger to Rivers to Manning. In minutes.

I have my doubts about this deal for the Giants. The qualities they see as extraordinary in Manning—which Accorsi described to me as the charismatic, clutch and leaderish "it" factor (something he also detailed at length to me in the magazine this week in a Rivers profile of mine, as well as the ability to lift the players around him) are just as present in Rivers.

But at the same time, how can you not love Manning? Great player, leader and teammate. Might be as good as his brother. For what the Giants gave, though, he'd better be. Accorsi said giving the one in 2005 "didn't bother me at all. When you think somebody is going to be as good as we think Eli's going to be, you pay the price you have to pay."

When Accorsi got home, after midnight, he was still wired from the day. He flipped on the TV. Maybe a good ball game would calm him. But his

MLB "Extra Innings" was dark; the last game on the pay baseball package, Seattle-Texas, was long over. "I just stared at the TV, trying to reconstruct the day. Amazing. Just amazing."

Accorsi didn't want to make this about himself, but exactly 21 years earlier he had been the Baltimore general manager who picked John Elway when Elway said he would never play for the team. Sound familiar? He couldn't keep Elway then. He had to get Manning now.

"Destiny owes me one," Accorsi said.

And that's the Weird Quarterback Tale of '04.

How many times can you look back at a deal like this one, with all its various permutations, and think: It worked out well for each team?

The Giants surrendered too much in draft pick compensation for my taste, but they got their man—and Eli Manning delivered a Super Bowl win three seasons ago with one of the best postseasons a quarterback has ever played. Mission accomplished.

The Steelers, oblivious to all the Giants-Chargers machinations, sat right where they were at No. 11. Roethlisberger fell into their lap. They've won two Super Bowls with him at quarterback.

The Chargers got their guy too. And Rivers has been terrific the past four years since taking over for Drew Brees; he just hasn't won the big one. Yet. ●

I think I'm no golf scribe, but an 81 at Bethpage Black is absurd. That's what Ben Roethlisberger shot there in June 2009, playing alongside Michael Jordan and Justin Timberlake. With Rocco Mediate on his bag, Big Ben, a three handicap, turned in a 39 on the back nine, with birdies on numbers 10 and 15. I walked that course during the 2009 U.S. Open—having seen the acres of sand and long meadows of deep grass, not to mention the ridiculously long holes like the 525-yard par-4 7th (with a dogleg, no less), I have to say I was fairly impressed with number 7's game.

MMQB Classic November 5, 2001

He Makes a Rather Good Color Man

The *CBS Evening News* anchorman sounded right at home in his debut as a pro football broadcaster

Between 1972 and '85, NFL coaches Mike Shanahan, Brad Childress and Sean Payton all played quarterback at that football mecca, Eastern Illinois University.

One of the things I've loved about Monday Morning Quarterback is that most Sundays the column just happens. When I wake up on Sunday morning, I know what some elements of the column will be, but I have no clue what the lead will be. Like the time I walked into the Giants Stadium press box nine years ago to cover a Cowboys-Giants game, and as I headed to my seat, I saw a very well-known national newsman in the radio booth. Now that's a column.

Midway through the third quarter in the Dallas Cowboys Radio Network booth high above the Giants Stadium turf, play-by-play man Brad Sham asked one of his analysts what he thought the Giants would do on first-and-10 from the Dallas 34.

"I think they're going long," his graying color man said. "I think they'll go for it."

Kerry Collins dropped back and threw a 34-yard strike to Joe Jurevicius. Touchdown.

On the next possession, three plays later, Sham wondered aloud what the Cowboys would do on third-and-seven from the Giants' 48. "Button hook," the analyst said. "Ten, maybe 11 yards downfield." Clint Stoerner dropped back. Joey Galloway streaked up the left side and curled back in, just as Stoerner fired the ball into him. Completion.

Twenty-four yards.

"He's got Galloway on a button-hook!" Sham shouted.

With 4:32 left in the game and the Giants threatening to score the go-ahead touchdown at the Dallas three-yard line, the color man said the Cowboys sure needed a turnover right now.

"Dayne on the carry. . . . " Sham said. *"Fumble!"*

Dallas ball. In came Ryan Leaf for his first Dallas outing. Second down. Leaf fades back. "Turn it loose, Leaf!" yelled the analyst. Leaf, as if on cue, wound up and threw a bullet to Rocket Ismail.

Now you know about Dan Rather's NFL broadcasting debut.

"You are being wasted in news," the permanent color guy, Babe Laufenberg, said. "You've got to come over to sports!"

"Can we take you to Atlantic City with us?" Sham asked.

I'm in the Comfort Inn near the BWI Airport. I open the wrapped soap, use it for a morning shower, and put it back on the soap dish. I'd say the soap is about half as thick as the bar you'd buy in the store. This bar could last 10 or 12 days, easily. And so the next morning, when I step into the shower, I find the bar's been taken away. This happens all the time. Hotels of America, I ask you: Why do you waste soap like that? Why not simply put another wrapped bar near the sink, and if the customer for some strange reason wants to throw away the lightly used soap, he or she can do so and open a new bar.

I listened to most of the Cowboys' 27–24 overtime loss to the Giants, with guest analyst Rather, the 71-year-old *CBS Evening News* anchor, on a wireless headset in the press box. And let me tell you: Rather was good. Very good. I'm serious when I say this: Dan Rather should do this more often. The credibility he brings with those pipes is already formidable. But he knows the game from couch-potatoing on most fall Sundays through the years, and he has an excellent sense of the flow of the game. He's not intrusive, and he knows when to shut up, two skills that a lot of color men have never mastered.

This was already a state-of-the-art broadcast team anyway. Sham, who's a Cowboys guy without being a homer in any way, has a homespun but newsy way about him. Laufenberg, a former Dallas backup quarterback, gives a player's perspective; like Sham, he isn't afraid to knock the Cowboys when they do something dumb, like going for broke on third-and-25 when they were trying to protect a late lead, which resulted in a Clint Stoerner interception. "That's a horrible play call," Laufenberg said. "You don't put the football into Clint Stoerner's hands on third-and-25," he said.

This was Rather's first football in about 45 years, he told me at halftime. "I did the University of Houston's play-by-play in the mid-'50s for

"One of the great things about being in Paris is nobody cares about the Lions."

—Detroit vice chairman Bill Ford Jr., speaking at an auto show in France in September 2002.

four years." His $85-a-week radio job was sup-
plemented by the $20 he got for Cougars' play-
by-play. ("That was the difference in income in
those days," Rather said.) Maybe he was rusty,
but he fit like the three-year-old sneakers under
your bed. Rather blended in, giving respect to
Sham and Laufenberg while rarely intruding.
But if Rather had something to say, he said it,
sometimes forcefully.

Late in the first half, with the Cowboys trying
to add to a 24–7 lead, Laufenberg said they ought
to be positioning themselves for a field goal. Rather jumped in quickly. "No," he said. "Go for the
TD. Go for the kill shot on them. It's not greedy.
You have a chance to put them away. Seven more
points and it's adios."

Ratherisms:

• On the Cowboys celebrating once they
jumped to a 17–7 lead: "You don't taunt the al-
ligator till you cross the creek, and they still have
plenty of creek to cross."

• At halftime, with the Giants down 24–7:
"You play this poorly in New York, and you're
lucky you don't get run out of the county."

• After a Dallas interception was returned for
a touchdown: "Did you see Giants coach Jim Fassel? He leaped up like somebody stuck him with
a hat pin."

Want to know why
Brian Dawkins
was so eager to
leave the Eagles
in 2009? Base
salary Dawkins
earned his last
three seasons in
Philadelphia:
$6.2 million.
Guaranteed
money Dawkins
will earn in
Denver in
two years:
$7.2 million.

• On early Dallas domination: "The Cowboys have beaten the Giants like a rented mule."

Cute stuff. Rather also told his Texas audience what it was like to be a New Yorker these days. One upshot of the adjustment in Rather's world is that he can't get mail right now due to anthrax concerns. When the Cowboys were sending him press material to study for his game broadcast, they had to express-mail the packet to a friend in New Jersey who hand-delivered it to Rather. "More pleases, thank-yous and pardon-mes have been said since September 11 than had been said in the last 20 years," he said. "How can the tragedy not have affected you in a deep and abiding way?"

From 5-13-02:
I think the
Chargers play in
L.A. by 2008.

He paused near the top of the booth during a halftime break when I asked him, "How's your life going these days?"

"Weird," he said. "Complicated. But everybody's life is, isn't it?" Which is why, when he looked out to a perfect blue sky and a full stadium on a crisp autumn day in the second half, he seemed so incredibly happy just to be there. "What a wonderful football afternoon this is," he said. For him, especially.

The one thing I do remember about that time in our history was the politeness in public and the nonpartisanship in politics. I wish we could get both back. ●

Ten Things I Think I Think

Commissioner For a Day

These would be my first 10 orders of business if I were the all-knowing, all-powerful king of the NFL

1. GIVE EACH TEAM AT LEAST ONE POSSESSION IN OVERTIME. The modification voted in by the owners last spring—each team gets a possession, barring a touchdown or defensive safety on the first possession of OT—is a start, but it's not enough. And it's only for the 2010 playoffs, which certainly won't do. There are 16 games in a season. To the teams that are contending for playoff spots, each, obviously, is precious. Remember the 2008 Jets-Pats game, in Foxborough? Two teams tied for first place in the AFC East lit each other up through regulation. The fourth quarter ended with the score tied at 31–31. Watching the game, you knew that the winner of the coin toss was going to march down the field through the papier-maché defense of the other side and win the game. The Jets won the toss. Brett Favre paraded the Jets to a field goal. Matt Cassel, who had driven the Pats

In 2008 the Giants named Snausages (I just love that brand name) the official dog snack of the team. For every third down New York converted, Snausages donated $100 to New York Pet Rescue in Larchmont, N.Y. Think of that promotion: Someone actually had to think of it, present it at a Snausages board meeting, sell it to the Giants, and do it with a straight face.

offense to a 511-yard night, never had a shot. New York won the game and the division. New England lost and ended up missing the playoffs. You can't tell me that if the Patriots had won the toss that they wouldn't have won the game. And by the way, I don't care if only 43% of the overtime games are won on the first possession by the team winning the toss. Fair is fair. And fair is not allowing one team to have the ball by virtue of the toss of a coin, and the other team quite possibly not touching the ball at all.

2. ELIMINATE TIES. Play overtime clockless, with at least one possession per team, until there's a winner. Ties are stupid.

3. NEVER, EVER, EVER, EVER INCREASE THE SCHEDULE BEYOND 16 REGULAR-SEASON GAMES. One of the weirdest things I've ever done in MMQB was to run the name of every starter who'd missed a game in the first quarter of the 2007 season due to injury. The list was something like 210 players long. Then after Week 7 of the 2008 season, I took another look at the casualties. Lost were reigning MVP and offensive player of the year Tom Brady; defensive player of the year Bob Sanders; nine more starting quarterbacks (including Tony Romo and Carson Palmer) and 17 other Pro Bowl participants from the year before, not to mention 43 offensive

Nnamdi Asomugha and Iheanyi Uwaezuoke are cousins.

skill players. I did this to show how dangerous a game this is, and how much of a crapshoot it would be to play one or two extra games. I fear that in some cases—many cases—the luckiest team, the least-injured team, might win a playoff game or the whole ball of wax. I'll tell you what's interesting: You talk to coaches and personnel people off the record, and almost every one will tell you what a dumb idea this is because of how players get bigger, stronger and faster every year, and how the collisions just get more violent, and the human body isn't meant to take what they're put through now, never mind with a couple of extra real games. You know why you won't hear coaches say anything? Because it's not the company line. But I did get this gem from Ravens center Matt Birk: "When I hear people in the league talk about 18 games, I cringe. I don't how we make it through 16, the way this game tests you mentally and physically. Sixteen games is plenty."

4. FIX THE PRESEASON BY PLAYING TWO REGULAR PRESEASON GAMES, AND TWO SCRIMMAGES USING THE BOTTOM 50 PLAYERS ON THE 80-MAN CAMP ROSTER. No coach wants his trusted veterans to play in more than a dozen series in the preseason, so you get those in during the two real exhibitions. In the other two preseason

My 10 alltime favorite movies

1. *Casablanca*

2. *North by Northwest*

3. *High Noon*

4. *Animal House*

5. *Field of Dreams*

6. *Best in Show*

7. *The Godfather*

8. *The Princess Bride*

9. *Gran Torino*

10. *Saving Private Ryan*

Honorable mention: *Christmas Vacation*, which the King family still watches once a year, like a bunch of howling fools.

"I think the Internet is like television in 1948, with infinite potential. The Internet is going to completely change the way commerce is done in the whole world."

—New England owner Bob Kraft in October 1999. (Talk about prophetic.)

games, you play controlled scrimmages in NFL-hungry parts of the country, charge $10 a head, and have backups and rookies fight it out for roster spots. The Detroit Lions, for instance, would meet the Indianapolis Colts between the two cities in South Bend, and the next week the Lions would bus to Toledo to play the Cleveland Browns. The Cincinnati Bengals and Tennessee Titans would meet in Louisville, the Bengals and Washington Redskins in Morgantown. You get the idea. Only the Seattles and Arizonas would be geographically disadvantaged by having to fly everywhere. But the NFL, after its recent personal-seat-license black eyes in Dallas and New York, needs to do something fan-friendly. And $10 tickets, plus crowd-pleasing, meet-the-players stuff after the scrimmage, would be the kind of thing a smart league would do. And the $1.5 million or $2 million per team it would cost to eliminate one home preseason game per team? Ask Giants owner John Mara if he would have paid $1.5 million to have had defensive end Osi Umenyiora for the 2008 season, or ask Denver's Pat Bowlen if he wouldn't have done the same to have had defensive end Ebenezer Ekuban for the 2007 season, or Atlanta's Arthur Blank vis-à-vis quarterback Michael Vick in 2003. You get the point. The way players train in the off-season, it's just not essential for them to play more than a few series in the preseason.

5. TAKE CARE OF THE OLD PLAYERS BY STARTING A FUND USING ONE-HALF OF 1% OF THE NFL'S GROSS REVENUES ANNUALLY FOR THEIR CARE. The medical and mental care benefits for retired NFL players are a disgrace. You don't need me to recite chapter and verse why, or how we got to this point. The way to fix this is simple: In the next CBA negotiations between the owners and players—the commish has to convince each side to give one-quarter of 1% of their gross revenues to a fund to take care of retired players in perpetuity. So instead of players getting 60% of the gross revenue, they'd get 59.75%—and they'd be able to sleep at night. As would the owners, who'd get 39.75% instead of 40. That little half-a-percentage-point would rake in about $35 million annually, which, added to the current pie, would go a long way toward making the golden years at least tolerable for the old Sunday warriors.

6. MANDATE THAT ALL COACHES AND PLAYERS, ONCE TRAINING CAMP BEGINS, SPEND THREE HOURS A WEEK WITH THE FANS. Some players do it willingly. Derrick Mason of the Ravens would wait out the last autograph-seeker, for instance. I've

In the Quiet Car aboard an Amtrak Metroliner, a man across the aisle tapped me on the shoulder while I was typing on my PowerBook. "Could you keep it down a little?" he said. "Huh?" I said. "The typing," he said. "You're pounding the keyboard." Now *that's* what I call a Quiet Car.

I think I knew
my postgame
interview with
Kansas City
linebacker
Derrick Thomas
13 minutes after
Jacksonville's
21–16 win over
the Chiefs
in September 1998
would not go well
when I asked him
how he felt his
matchup with Tony
Boselli went.
"Peter," he said,
with eyes of
daggers, "don't
ask me any more
dumb questions."

seen Buffalo Bills players mingle with fans at a western New York bar during training camp—and not shoo them away. You know how much that means to fans, and how much it translates into good faith and fans getting back the love they give so freely to the teams that they support? Imagine multiplying that times 2,000, every week. That's human-touch marketing. I hate to be arbitrary and despotic, but most players aren't going to do this consistently unless it's mandated by the league.

7. MOVE JACKSONVILLE, BUT NOT TO WHERE YOU THINK. Make them the London Jaguars. Come on. Jacksonville just never became Atlanta Jr., which the league surely thought would happen when it committed to putting a franchise there nearly 17 years ago. Still looks like Hartford with palm trees to me. Nothing wrong with that, but business didn't grow the way everyone thought it would in that area. There's got to be some radical thought at 280 Park Avenue. It's coming. Why not now? Why not a market that would bend over backward for the NFL? The NFL would be the first sports league to plant a team overseas. And by the way, the first player or coach or owner to complain about the six-hour flight (or nine hours if you're the Seahawks) to a road game? I'll order them traded to Hamilton of the Canadian loop.

8. TAKE THE PRO BOWL VOTE AWAY FROM THE FANS . . . AND AWAY FROM THE PLAYERS. Both stink at this. How insane is it that fans vote for guards? And how much time do players really spend trying to get it right? Really insane, and two minutes. Here's the new voting formula I'd make law: Each team would have three voters—the offensive coordinator, defensive coordinator and pro scout. There are, then, 48 voters per conference, voting for 27 spots: 11 offensive starters, a kicker, a punter, a return man, a special-teams player and 12 defensive starters (accounting for four defensive linemen and four linebackers because of the 3–4 and 4–3 defenses). Most of the politics would be removed. Ties would be broken by Cris Collinsworth. Just kidding. Maybe.

9. MAKE THE THANKSGIVING DAY GAMES REWARDS FOR PLAYOFF TEAMS THE PREVIOUS YEAR. O.K., the real motivation is to get Detroit out of our homes while the turkey's being served every year. (No it isn't. But you have to admit that you dread the Lions game on Thanksgiving, and have for some time.) I don't like the advantage a team like Dallas gets on Thanksgiving. Each year from 2005 to '09, Dallas hosted a Sunday game before Thanksgiving and then the Thursday game on the holiday. In those five years, the Cowboys are 9–1 in those

From 8-28-06: One of us, either Jerry Jones or me, is going to be egg-faced about Tony Romo's taking the Cowboys quarterback job, by virtue of performance and not injury, from Drew Bledsoe sometime this year. I said on TV that Dallas would seriously consider such a move in-season. Jones shot me full of holes this way: "The media has really got it figured out. They've got to fill air time and create interest and all. But it's so far away from any real meat or any real substance."

Romo was starting by Week 7.

eight games, scoring 137 more points than their foes. And then they have a mini-bye, with three extra days off for the players to heal. When you have this built into your schedule every year, it's a pretty sweet advantage.

10. REALIGN, AGAIN—IN PART TO BE GREEN. I'd grandfather in only one weird situation—Dallas in the NFC East—because there's no logical place for the Cowboys to go, and because they've been in the same division with New York, Washington and Philadelphia for 42 years. The eight divisions almost got fixed on the last go-round in 2002. Almost. But Indianapolis is not a Southern team. Indy, Baltimore and Miami need to make a three-team trade. The Colts would join Cincinnati, Cleveland and Pittsburgh in the AFC North, the most eco-friendly division in all of pro sports—there'd be no road trip longer than 360 miles. The Bengals and the Browns would have no more than a 4.5-hour bus trip to any of the three other cities in the division. Miami goes to the AFC South, where soon enough the Dolphins would have an I-95 rivalry with Jacksonville (assuming the Jags stay in Florida). And Baltimore, a quasi-Rust Belt, quasi-Megalopolis city, would fit perfectly with two Amtrak trips to the Jets and Pats and a quick hop to Buffalo. The NFC can stand pat.

Cardinals quarterback Derek Anderson wore a size 17 shoe at age 10.

MMQB Classic December 29, 2008

Why Peyton Manning Is My 2008 MVP

It seems like a tough call, but once you hear what the Colts quarterback went through, it's a no-brainer

Peyton Manning's reputation has never been as a gutsy, he'd-play-with-a-bone-sticking-out-of-his-leg warrior. I'm thinking that could change after 2008.

For my 2008 MVP, I'm going with James Harrison at five, DeAngelo Williams four, Chad Pennington three, Matt Ryan two. And Peyton Manning one.

I have been leaning toward Manning for the past four or five weeks, because I've felt—particularly in rallying the Colts from season-saving 15- and 17-point late-game deficits to beat Minnesota and Houston early—the Colts would have been well below .500 without him. Manning never had a running game all season to help him; the Colts' 3.4-yard average per rush was their lowest this decade. He started the season

"A versatile guy is a guy who can be very versatile."

—University of Texas defensive end/outside linebacker Brian Orakpo, who, in a press conference at the 2009 scouting combine, mentioned his versatility four times in a 90-second span.

more hurt than we knew (at least until now) and without his redoubtable center Jeff Saturday. The Colts went 3–4 through the end of October, but it would have been 1–6 without those comebacks over the Vikings and Texans. Then, with Manning finally getting his legs under him, the Colts rode a classic 9–0 Manning stretch to finish 12–4 and earn the fifth seed in the AFC playoffs.

The story of Manning's 11th season is a good one, one he hasn't told to anyone in my business—to the best of my knowledge. As usually happens with Manning, our conversation was going to be 10 or 20 minutes, but by the end, I had enough stuff for a couple of chapters of a book.

The story actually starts in Hawaii, at the Pro Bowl last year.

"I started to experience swelling in my knee at the Pro Bowl," Manning said. "I had two weeks off after the playoffs ended for us. Did nothing before Hawaii. Went to the beach, went to the Super Bowl, showed up in Hawaii, all of a sudden my knee swelled up like a grapefruit. The Chargers trainers bent over backwards, treating a player that's not even their player. They're supposed to be on vacation, and here they are, driving me all over the place to get an MRI. No big deal, I thought. I played the game, and after the game, the thing

The Jets' playoff game against the Raiders on Jan. 12, 2003, was their fourth visit to Oakland in 53 weeks.

is gone, it's dissipated throughout my body. Very strange. I get back in April, start lifting weights, it blew up again. Couldn't kneel on it. I had a good off-season, thought I threw it pretty good, and I had the knee drained maybe seven times. Two or three weeks later it'd come back. Let me go back to a conversation I had with Bill Parcells when we did a commercial for the Super Bowl. He advised me, 'Don't ever forget your legs. Legs, legs legs. Do your squats. That's so important as you get older.' And I worked on that hard.

"On Monday before camp [actually July 14, 10 days before training camp opened], my leg's on fire, it's red, I'm hurtin' bad. I fly to Indy right away and find out the fluid in there's infected. So they tell me, 'We're gonna remove your bursa sac. Pretty standard procedure.' Then the fluid starts to seep back."

Doctors couldn't stop the fluid from seeping into the knee. Ten days after surgery, the knee was still swollen. The Colts set a deadline of Wednesday, July 30, to decide whether to have another procedure called "quilting" done. In quilting, a surgeon stitches the skin down to shut off the suspected flow of any infected fluid.

Now came the cloak-and-dagger stuff. Manning couldn't fly because of the risks of swelling and infection. So the Colts flew orthopedist-to-

In January 2007, my Continental flight to Newark was landing when the flight attendant said, "Ladies and gentlemen, we have quite a few passengers with tight flight connections. We would appreciate it if your final destination is Newark that you wait on board until those passengers have a chance to leave the aircraft." So I waited until the last person was off. "Sir," the flight attendant said, "you will have to leave now. Are you waiting for something?" "Well, you told me not to get off till the people with tight connections got off," I said. "Wow," she said. "Nobody usually pays attention to those announcements."

the-stars James Andrews (and one or two other experts) into Colts camp in Terre Haute, Ind., to examine him. He consulted with Giants team physician Russell Warren.

"All of them say the same thing: 'You've got to do something about it,'" Manning told me. "I agreed. My biggest fear was the Saturday night before we play the Patriots in November, it's gonna happen again."

So the second surgery was set for July 31 at 6 a.m. Manning was told it'd take about 30 minutes to sew about 20 sutures in the knee. The Colts had a car set to pick Manning up to take him home at 9 a.m.

He woke up at 5 p.m.

There weren't 20 sutures implanted. Doctors had to use 80.

And the surgery didn't take 30 minutes. It took three hours.

"They didn't have a choice," Manning said. "There was so much fluid, the pockets were so big, that they had to use 80."

The knee stayed wrapped on Thursday, Friday and Saturday. On Sunday, Colts director of rehabilitation Erin Barill came to Manning's house to check on how the knee was healing. "He warned me the knee does not look good," Manning said. "And he said, 'Do you want to see it?'"

Of course he did. "Funny thing was, I was getting ready to watch the Colts-Redskins Hall of Fame game. Weird. I have never watched the Colts play on TV, ever. And then I get ready to see what the knee looks like."

Drumroll. Barill took the wrap off.

"I looked down, and my knee looked like a brain after surgery. You know how they show you pictures of a brain in science class? That's what this was—swollen, ugly. I kind of got my hopes up, but it was disgusting. Mangled, in layers, dimples all over it. It didn't look good at all. My heart just sank. I was nervous and scared. It was so new to me. Some of these guys playing in the NFL have surgery all the time. Not me. The only surgery I'd ever had was for a deviated septum my sophomore year in high school. Here I have one July 14, then another one two weeks later. Uncharted waters for me."

This thought occurred to me then: How in the world did he, and the Colts, keep this whole thing so under wraps?

Manning had his own anal traits, plus the never-ending Brett Favre retirement saga, to thank for that. "I'm one of those guys who never wants to be on the injury report," he said. "I don't want people to say, 'What's wrong with your ankle or your knee or whatever?' I don't want my

From 1-13-03:
Amos Zereoue is
the AFC's budding
Tiki Barber.

opponents to know anything. When I see a corner who's got a bad ankle, I say, 'Let's check this thing out in the game.' Plus, the whole Favre thing was dominating the news. Nobody had time to report anything else.

"It was the most miserable training camp. I'd do the rehab in my dorm to stay out of the way of people at camp. The best thing that happened was I had a video machine in my room. I was watching. . . . I was waiting all day for the practice tape. I was dying. I just wanted to see the tape."

Days turned into weeks. The Colts originally said Manning's injury was a four-to-six-week job, and when he got close to the six-week anniversary, Manning still wasn't working out.

"Remember what Parcells told me. 'Legs, legs, legs.' Well, I lost all my strength in my left leg, and you don't want to create an imbalance in your legs, so I couldn't do much with my right leg either. But all the range of motion in my left leg was gone. Could I get to where I can drop and run? I had no idea. I really did not know. All I had ever known, every year in camp, was to take every rep, every practice. Now I get no reps in camp. The biggest thing as we got close to the season was I didn't think I could move the way I wanted to. I'll never be mistaken for Donovan McNabb or my

Want to make Giants running back Brandon Jacobs happy? Serve him some nice lasagna with a touch of nutmeg.

dad [mobile ex-Saints QB Archie Manning]. And my balance was a problem. I couldn't finish the throws." Making it worse was the absence of long-time center Saturday with a knee injury; he knew the hieroglyphic-type Colts offense as well as Manning. Now Indianapolis had to get seventh-round rookie Jamey Richard, a college guard, ready to face, in order, Tommie Harris, Kevin and Pat Williams, and John Henderson. Before the first game, instead of spending an extra half-hour or two a day working the legs, he was on the practice field and in the meeting room with Richard, teaching him the idiosyncrasies of being the Colts center.

Feeling weak, Manning had no impact on a 29–13 opening loss to Chicago. In Week 2 at Minnesota, the Vikes led 15–0 midway through the third quarter. "We're down 15–0, thinking about being 0–2, and knowing we've got Jacksonville the next week. Not good," Manning said. He led two touchdown drives, with a two-point conversion on the second, to tie it. "Probably the biggest play of the game, third-and-10 on the 50 [actually third-and-nine at the Minnesota 49], I get Reggie Wayne on a post route from the slot, ball rushes right past the DB's ear into Reggie. That told me, 'I can still make these throws. If I keep rehabbing, I can make it back. I still have it.'" Gain of 20. The Colts won on a field goal.

I think Penn State was insane in December 2008, giving a three-year contract extension to an 81-year-old coach with health problems. Why was there no one at this august institution who could tell a man who the school isn't positive can even *stand* on the sideline every week that it was time to step down? Can anyone who bleeds Nittany blue honestly tell me that Joe Paterno has the energy to outrecruit coaches 40 years his junior for the best football players in the country?

Manning struggled again the next week; Indy lost to Jacksonville. "The next week, Houston's got us 27–10 midway through the fourth quarter. It is not looking good. Lotta people thinking, 'Here come the Texans'—they finished 8–8 the year before, their crowd's fired up, they're inspired to win after Hurricane Ike. But it's your job to play till the final seconds. I throw a touchdown pass to Tom Santi that looks like a stat-padder. Then [Gary] Brackett takes a fumble back for a touchdown." Luckily for the Colts, Houston quarterback Sage Rosenfels was awful that day and handed the Colts a touchdown and a short field late. Manning threw the winning touchdown pass to Wayne off that short field. Colts, 31–27.

They could easily have been 0–4. But 18 points in the last 20 minutes at Minnesota, and 21 points in the last five at Houston, and the season was saved.

What was bugging Manning at that point, even at 2–2, was the amount of time he had to spend every week in rehab and rebuilding the strength in his legs. Instead of coming in early to watch tape or talk to a coach before the morning meetings, Manning had to be in by 6:30 for an hour of rehab five days a week and spend another hour postpractice doing the same. He still did most of his other work, but not as much of the on-field stuff with his receivers that he did ordinarily. Combine that with zero reps in training camp for a guy who craves them, and you see why he was treading water—10 touchdowns, nine picks, a 3–4 record after an ugly Monday night loss at Tennessee—through two months.

"It just sucked up all my energy," he said. "My goal has always been to avoid the trainers' room, and now, for the first time in my whole career, I'm going in every morning before meetings, challenging my preparation time. But after a couple of months of doing that—after the Tennessee game, I didn't have to go into the trainers room anymore. I felt right. But at that point, we're 3–4, and we all but ruled out winning the division. Tennessee wasn't gonna collapse. The biggest problem with New England coming up, Pittsburgh on the road, San Diego on the road, was avoiding sitting around saying, 'Boy, we are in trouble.' It was like, 'Are we going to say it's just not our year, wait till next year, or are we gonna do something about it?' The other thing people don't think about is we've got a lot of second-, third- fourth-year players, and we'd started the last three years 13–0, 9–0 and 7–0, and these guys are going, 'What the hell is going on?' But as Tony

During training camp in 2008 I dined with then-Browns G.M. Phil Savage on the patio of the Moosehead Saloon, a pleasant tavern on the border of Westlake and Bay Village on the west side of Cleveland. We sat on a cool, breezy, clear night for a couple of hours. Servers swarmed our table pleasantly and efficiently. Collectively we had a large order of home-baked potato chips, two ice teas (his), three Heineken Lights (mine), two megasalads (one with roast turkey, one with chicken), two orders of whole wheat Texas Toast and coffee. The bill came: $36.08. I thought: Isn't traveling wonderful?

All-over body-
tattooed young
lady to the clerk in
the Marriott City
Center gift shop in
Minneapolis one
Saturday morning
in October 2007:
"Can I get change
for a $20?" Clerk:
"Let me see if I
have it. How do
you want it?"
Tatwoman: "Can
I get five fives?
Four or five fives,
I'm not sure, you
know." That really
happened.

[Dungy] told 'em, this is what the NFL is all about."

As November dawned, the Colts knew they might have to go 8–1 or even 9–0 the rest of the way to make the playoffs. Manning, finally feeling good, got his team on a run.

"I truly believe it is no coincidence we have gone on the winning streak since then," Manning said.

Now on to the MVP issue. My take is that Manning was the keystone to this team's starting 3–4 instead of being out of it at 1–6. In the final nine games, Manning's 9–0 record led all NFL quarterbacks, Manning's 72% accuracy led all NFL quarterbacks, and Manning's 17-to-3 touchdown-to-interception (plus-14) ratio led all NFL quarterbacks.

He completed 21 of 29 to beat New England in Week 9. He got a little lucky with some Ben Roethlisberger turnovers the next week at Pittsburgh, but he also threw three of the 12 touchdown passes the Steelers allowed all season. His running game managed 154, 91, 90, 57, 106 and 105 yards over the next six games, but he had enough in the tank to win each one without much of a ground alternative.

In Sunday's Dungy special of a finale (the starters play a series or three), Manning played long enough to exceed 4,000 yards in a season for the ninth time. He went 7 for 7. Five months after recoiling in shock at the sight of his grotesque knee, he finished his most unlikely great season as an NFL quarterback.

So the Colts finished 12–4. It's not as stunning as the 11–5 of the Dolphins or Falcons, to be sure. You could argue—and you might win—that Miami without Pennington and Atlanta without Matt Ryan would have been 5–11 or worse. But I simply will not accept that coaches who proved themselves very resourceful (Tony Sparano, Mike Smith) would have been hapless without their quarterbacks. Miami would have played Chad Henne earlier. Atlanta would have ridden Michael Turner to a few wins. Indy? Without Manning, I say a team that ran the ball in quicksand the way the Colts did would have been 4–12.

"This has been my most rewarding regular season, because of what we've all been faced with here," Manning said. "I've been proud to be on this team. Guys dug deep. I dug deep."

Come to think of it, this MVP pick's not that tough a call.

If you want to bash Manning for not winning enough of the Big Ones, go ahead. But don't ever bash him about what's inside of him. ●

A plea by Bobby Mack of Fort Walton Beach, Fla., from May 2003: "Hey, please, don't call the Dolphins football team 'Fish.' Yes, I know all you sports broadcasters call them fish, but dolphins are marine mammals, not fish. That animal is plainly a marine mammal wearing a football helmet. Calling them fish is wrong, kind of like calling you guys 'journalists.'" Touché.

A Matter of Perspective

I met Mike McGuire by chance;
he soon became a very important
person in my column and in my life

In 1969, when Falcons president Rich McKay was 10 years old, he and his brother got a new babysitter. Their dad, John, coached USC at the time, and he had perfected the practice of taking the newest, youngest guy on his staff and making him the boys' babysitter. The McKay boys liked the new babysitter. He didn't just stick them in front of the TV. He paid attention to them and played with them. Who was he? Joe Gibbs.

One of the luckiest things that ever happened to me was buying a ticket to St. Louis Cardinals game five years ago, sitting down and falling into conversation with a complete stranger. That complete stranger has become a good friend and a familiar name to regular readers of my column. God doesn't make them better than Mike McGuire.

We interrupt this tour of NFL training camps to bring you reality. I want to take you into Mike McGuire's world.

Last Monday night I took in a baseball game, as I occasionally do on my tour of NFL camps. I walked up to the ticket window at Busch Stadium and bought an infield box seat for Marlins-Cards. Next to me sat a 30ish man in an Albert Pujols T-shirt and a St. Louis cap. We didn't say much to each other. There was a family in front of us, though, with a couple of young boys intensely interested in the game. After each starting pitcher got a hit in his first at bat, I turned to my seat-mate and said, "When's the last time you ever saw the two starting pitchers get hits their first time up?" And the 10-year-old kid in front of us turned around and said, "And they got 'em off each other!"

Sometimes kids say the darnedest things. We both laughed.

I noticed my neighbor was a great fan and very polite. We started talking football, because he was a huge Rams fan. He lived in Germany with his wife and five kids and was back in the States at Fort Leonard Wood in Missouri for two months to be trained in leadership-building for his Army job.

His name was Mike McGuire. He's an Army sergeant, first class, having recently been promoted to command a platoon of 30 men. They're kids, really. He's 34. Most of his troops are between 18 and 20.

He told me he'll take his platoon to Iraq in early November.

"What will you do there?" I said.

"IED-hunting," he said. "Improvised Explosive Devices. Our job is to find them and neutralize them so they don't kill people."

Whoa now. I keep score at baseball games. I

"You want to know the 13 scariest words in professional football this year? 'For more on the Cowboys, let's go to Ed Werder at Valley Ranch.'"

—*Tampa Tribune* NFL writer Ira Kaufman, on the team's Terrell Owens soap opera in 2008.

If you haven't lived in the Boston area, it's tough to explain the looniness that occurs when the Red Sox are in the playoffs, especially against the New York Darth Vaders. In October 2004 Boston mayor Thomas Menino told the assembled press: "Lord, it's been 86 years. Hear our prayer. Make us world champions." Mayor Menino went on to say: "Much like a cookie, I believe the Yankee Dynasty will crumble. The results will be delicious for Red Sox fans everywhere."

always have. But now I have to stop and stare at Mike McGuire.

"You mean you're the guys who search for those huge bombs planted on the side of the road? Those bombs that kill people over there every day?"

"Yes sir," he said.

"My God. I can't imagine that. The danger . . . " My voice trailed off.

"There are dangers," he said. "We know that. But the job has to be done. We're doing what has to be done."

"How do you do it?"

"Well, we drive along and look for anything that looks out of place. Maybe it's some gravel that looks too neat. Maybe it's a sign in Arabic that tells the locals to stay away from a spot. We're trained in what to look for, but it's not an exact science."

I tried to think of how to put this nicely. But there was no way.

"I read about people dying every day because of these devices. Aren't you scared?"

"Well, you try not to think of that. I have 30 kids in my platoon to worry about. I'm not scared for me, really. I'm scared for those kids. They're so young. You feel like you want to protect them. It's my job. Even when I see them out at night and maybe they're drinking, I say, 'I'm calling your mom.' I tease 'em like that."

I don't know what else to say. We talk baseball for a while, and then we talk about the Rams. "I love St. Louis," he said. "It's my home, and I'm really into the Rams. Greatest show on turf. Hope I get a chance to see them before I go back the first of October."

I made a mental note to tell the St. Louis organization about this guy. They should invite him and his dad to a game. Heck, Mike Martz ought to bring him in to talk to the team. Here's a guy whose biggest thrill is to see the Rams whip up on someone, while he's literally going to be laying his life on the line. We took a photo together, finished watching the game, exchanged e-mail addresses and said goodbye.

All I could think of that night was that I was going to watch a football team run through a practice the next day, and Mike McGuire was going to learn leadership skills at an Army base so he could lead 30 kids in the most dangerous job on the planet. I'd be going to a lot more football games. Would Mike McGuire? And he was so businesslike about it. I suppose he had to be, but what a burden.

St. Louis, Long Island, Denver. My merry-go-round kept spinning.

At the start of the 2008 season the Colts were on track to devote $81.3 million of their 2009 salary cap to their seven highest-paid players. That would leave an estimated $40.7 million of the cap to be shared by the remaining 46 players on the active roster, eight practice-squad players and however many injured-reserve players. Salary-cap average for the seven highest-paid players: $11,614,286. Salary-cap average for the rest: $678,333.

I think I wonder why everyone got so bent out of shape when Indianapolis was awarded the 2012 Super Bowl. Northern cities with domed stadiums that have lobbied hard for Super Bowls have always gotten Super Bowls. The Silverdome, the Metrodome, Ford Field and now Lucas Oil Stadium. Owners award Super Bowl sites. Sportswriters don't. Party-planners don't. Travel agents don't. And owners are always going to give a Super Bowl to an owner who builds a new stadium. One. That's it. It will never change. Nor should it.

Thursday morning, I opened *The New York Times* at the Westin in Denver.

14 MARINES KILLED BY ROADSIDE BOMB IN WEST IRAQ CITY, the headline said.

The story was stunning in its brutality.

"The Marines had been riding in an amphibious troop carrier . . . when the bomb exploded. The blast flipped the 25-ton troop carrier and caused it to burst into flames."

Inside the *Times* was another story about the fact that roadside bombs used by the enemy are growing in size and potency. "At least four Army bomb technicians have been killed by such hidden bombs this year," the story said.

I e-mailed Sergeant McGuire, asking him to call me on my cellphone. Around 5:30 that afternoon, he did.

"Hey," he said cheerfully. "How you doing?"

"Good," I said. "Are you O.K.?"

"Fine."

I asked him about the 14 dead Marines. When he hears about things like that, does he get concerned about his safety?

What a stupid question. But he answered it earnestly.

"I think about it," he said. "Mostly, I read about how it happened, to try to learn something about how to stop it, how to detonate the bombs that are there now. I try not to think about the people. If I think about the victims, well, that doesn't help me do my job. That gets pretty tough."

I commiserated with Sergeant McGuire. I told him to be careful and to keep in touch. I told him to get into a fantasy football league, and I'd give him all of my worthless tips.

Then he called the experience he was about to get in Iraq "the chance of a lifetime." And I thought: What a man.

I worry about McGuire, who was on his second long tour in Iraq in 2009 and was prepping for his third one as the paperback version of this book went to press this summer. Being an IED-wrangler is no way to live, and I can tell it's wearing on him. I feel it in his e-mails, which come about once a month. In March 2009 he lost another soldier to an IED blast.

"I am holding up well, staying busy," he e-mailed during his second tour. "One day all this madness will hit me I am sure. I don't know how I will react, but it is building up. Hard to be tough and the first sergeant when really all I want to do is see my family and grieve our fallen men. I guess when I return home and I'm sitting alone in the dark on my porch, I will remember them all and make peace with all this." God knows how. ●

There was a recurring ad on NESN in 2007 for Southwest Airlines introducing new service between Manchester, N.H., and Phoenix, one-way, for as low as $59. One Thursday that summer, in New York City to interview NFL commissioner Roger Goodell, I parked in a Manhattan garage, for two hours and 36 minutes. The fee? $59. What a country. You can fly 2,479 miles nonstop from the woods of New Hampshire to the desert of the southwest, or you can park your car in a microscopic spot in New York City for as long as it takes to have lunch. Same price.

Ten Things I Think I Think

Lords of the Sidelines

The right coach can make all the difference in the world: These are the 10 smartest hires of all time

1. PAUL BROWN, *1946, Browns.* A new league, the All-America Football Conference, was founded at war's end, and Cleveland owner Arthur McBride hired Brown to coach it. Seeing as he already was a legendary name in Ohio football because of high school and college success, the franchise was nicknamed after Brown. He delivered seven championships in his first 10 years at the helm of the Browns, including three in the NFL after the two leagues merged in 1950.

2. CHUCK NOLL, *1969, Steelers.* Team president Dan Rooney brought young Penn State coach Joe Paterno into his kitchen, gave him a home-cooked meal, and tried to sway him to jump to the Steelers. But Paterno had a good thing going in Happy Valley and didn't want to risk ruining his coaching future by taking a step down with the perennially last-place Steelers. Within 11 years, bridesmaid Noll delivered four Super Bowls.

Back in 2002 when Starbucks announced that it was phasing in Internet access in its stores, I remember thinking, This is trouble. This means I could actually live there.

3. GEORGE HALAS, *1920, 1933, 1946, 1958, Bears.* MVP of the 1919 Rose Bowl. Played 12 games in the Yankees outfield in 1919. Became player-coach of the Bears in 1920. Stripped Jim Thorpe on a running play in 1923 and ran 98 yards for a TD. And so forth. He went back and forth between owning and coaching the team and serving in the military in his next two stints. How about this for his final act as Bears icon: hiring Mike Ditka as coach in 1982.

4. VINCE LOMBARDI, *1959, Packers.* The Pack had gone 4–8, 3–9 and 1-10-1 in the three years before Lombardi's hiring. He coached there for nine years, winning the conference six times and the league five. Seems as if he also trails only God and Abraham Lincoln in books written about him.

5. BILL BELICHICK, *2000, Patriots.* Friends all over the league told owner Bob Kraft he was nuts for hiring the monosyllabic Belichick. Despite the ugly Spygate scandal, in his 10 years at the helm Belichick has repaid Kraft with an average of 12.6 regular- and playoff wins a season.

6. DON SHULA, *1963, Colts.* Shula was hired at 33 (much, as it turned out, to the chagrin of Johnny Unitas, who didn't like a kid telling him what to do) to replace Weeb Ewbank. In those days, teams played 14-game seasons, so it's fairly impressive that Shula went 71-23-4 in seven years honing his coaching craft before jumping to the Dolphins.

The Packers swept the Minnesota–Green Bay regular-season series in 2004 when Ryan Longwell kicked field goals at the final gun to win both games by three points. The Vikings swept the Minnesota–Green Bay regular-season series in 2005 when Paul Edinger kicked field goals at the final gun to win both games by three points.

After the Redskins scored their go-ahead TD against Arizona in the third quarter at FedEx Field on Sept. 8, 2002, a group of four black men called the Funky 4 began dancing in the end zone. They were dressed in some yellow-and-crimson garb that was supposed to have them look like Native Americans. Four black men, dressed as Native Americans, dancing to *Play That Funky Music (White Boy)*. Only in America.

7. BILL WALSH, *1979, 49ers.* When Paul Brown was looking to replace himself as coach in Cincinnati in 1976, he picked one offensive assistant, Tiger Johnson, over another, Bill Walsh. Nice pick, Coach. Johnson went 18–15 in three forgettable years. Walsh moved West, finally got his shot in 1979, and won three Super Bowls in 10 years.

8. JIMMY JOHNSON, *1989, Cowboys.* 1989: NFC East coaches lick lips at college guy coming into toughest division in football. 1994: NFC East coaches pass a collection plate, trying to raise money to get this crazy idiot out of the league after he wins his second Super Bowl with a small, fast defense that no team can match.

9. JOHN MADDEN, *1969, Raiders.* Like Shula, Madden coached his first NFL game at 33—and he had 100 wins by 42, when he left the coaching game forever. Madden figured out how to handle Al Davis, which most of his successors could never do. "I just talked to him," Madden said. "We'd argue, we'd talk, every day, for a long time."

10. TONY DUNGY, *2002, Colts.* Think of the history of the franchise when he arrived. The 13 previous coaches had gone 209-277-2, the franchise had moved, and Jim Mora had the best coaching moment when he squawked, "Playoffs? *Playoffs*!?" Dungy delivered five division titles and one championship in his first six years.

MMQB Classic November 27, 2000

Terrell Davis Battles a Mystery Injury

He had beaten many of the game's best defenders, but a bum knee was one obstacle he couldn't get around

On a cold, dreary, raining-sideways afternoon in the Pacific Northwest, I thought I was going to make Terrell Davis cry. One of the best backs of our day was trying passionately to play despite a chronic knee injury that showed up on zero X-rays.

Terrell Davis understands what the outside world must be thinking. The MRIs show nothing wrong with his left knee, shin, calf or ankle. Two orthopedic specialists who have examined him within the past two weeks can find nothing wrong with his left knee, shin, calf or ankle. Last Wednesday he flew to Oakland for the second exam, with Dr. Roger Mann, who found nothing structurally wrong and labeled the problem "idiopathic" or unexplained pain. Mann basically told Davis: You should be able to play. On Sunday former play-

Number of games it took Dan Marino to throw for 20,000 yards: 74.

Number of games it took Kurt Warner to throw for 20,000 yards: 76.

er Brent Jones stopped just short of saying Davis should suck it up and play, on the CBS telecast of Denver's 38–31 win against the Seahawks.

Davis feels the hot breath of the outside world, and he understands the warriors' code of the NFL. Play, damn it. Your team's season is on the line, with a playoff-type battle every Sunday.

"If I could play, believe me, I'd be playing," Davis said quietly but forcefully outside the Broncos' locker room after Sunday's game. "But there is a line a player has to know when you're dealing with injuries. Either you can play or you can't. And at this point, I just can't play."

He hasn't been talking much through his nightmare of a season—Sunday was his seventh missed game—but he agreed to discuss the injury with me in the dank hallway underneath Husky Stadium. The history: After working tirelessly to come back from 1999 ACL surgery, the '98 NFL and Super Bowl MVP returned for the Broncos' opener and suffered left foot and ankle sprains against the Rams. Since then, while continuing rehab work on his knee and ankle, he said intense pain has developed in the shin area of his left leg. "There's pain from the calf area to the area around the top of the ankle," he explained. The maddening thing, and the inexplicable thing, is how he was able to gut out a 33-carry game against the Jets on Nov. 5, and

"Coach Parcells gave us four things he wanted us to do that would help us make the team. One was, 'No mental mistakes.' One was, 'Be reliable' ... Uh, I forget what the other two were."

—Rookie Jets tackle Jason Fabini, praised by coach Bill Parcells for making zero mental errors, after a December 1998 game.

then play the following week against the Raiders, and since then, nothing.

"There's something seriously wrong in there, and I don't know what it is," Davis told me.

"People who know me know I've played with pain most of my career," he said. "Ankles, split ribs, shoulder . . ."

"Migraines," reminded Bronco p.r. aide Richard Stewart, standing nearby.

"Migraines," Davis added. "But this thing, whatever it is, is more severe. The encouraging thing after I saw the specialist this week was that they found nothing structurally wrong with the leg. That's good. But then I try to push off the leg"—he did it just then, trying to do a toe-raise with the left leg—"I can't push up. It's very, very painful. And if you can't do that, you can't play football. It's strange. It's frustrating."

Part of me wonders this, cynically: Davis got his big contract after his Super Bowl success, and maybe he doesn't have the motivation to work as hard as he did when he was a sixth-round pick fighting to make his mark. And with quarterback Brian Griese's gutty (some would stay stupidly so) performance two weeks ago—beating the Raiders with a third-degree shoulder separation—fresh in the team's collective mind, it's only natural for some in the organization to wonder if Davis is faking it.

At security checkpoints around the U.S. in the summer of 2004:

Newark: Shoes must be removed and sent through the X-ray machine.

San Francisco: "It is strongly recommended that you remove your shoes," a security woman said.

Los Angeles, Green Bay, Indianapolis: No one said a word about removing shoes.

Minneapolis: "Do I take my shoes off?" I asked the security man. He said he would advise I do.

Newark (again): I say: "Should I take my shoes off?" And the guy on the other side of the X-ray machine hand-waves me through. One airport, two rules.

My 10 alltime
favorite TV shows:

1. *Seinfeld*
Hello, Newman.

2. *Mister Ed*
Hello, Wilbur.

3. *The Sopranos*
Hello, Tony.

4. *Curb Your
Enthusiasm*
Susie is one great
TV character.

5. *The Dick Van
Dyke Show*
Loved Mel Cooley.

6. *The Wild Wild
West*
Every kid wanted
to be James West.

7. *Family Guy*
Brian the dog is
one of my favorite
TV characters.

8. *The Office*
If Andy Bernard
went to Cornell, I'm
dean at Harvard.

9. *House*
But I can't watch
the gory medical
scenes.

10. *Leave It to
Beaver*
Ward, don't be too
hard on the boys.

I don't know Davis well. I've never spent any extended time outside a locker room with him. But after talking to him Sunday night, I feel this way: We can't know what's in this man's body. We can't know his pain. It's so out of character for him to not play when all signs and doctors say he should play. I'm reminded of the J.R. Richard story, when the former Houston Astros pitcher kept telling everybody his back hurt and everybody kept telling him to stop whining, and then he was felled by a stroke. After much deliberation—and my basic faith in human beings until they do something to show that faith is unfounded—I believe Davis. I believe the Davis who looks me in the eye and swears he's hurt too badly to play.

This week Davis will get more treatment on the leg. He'll try to practice, though I doubt, with a game on the hard fake turf in New Orleans, he has much of a chance to play this week. Lucky for the Broncos, rookie Mike Anderson (971 yards through 10 games) is carrying a heavy load.

"I'm optimistic I'll be able to play again this year," Davis said. "But this is a strange injury. I don't know what more I can do."

Davis was never right again. Twenty months later, the knee forced him into a premature retirement at 29, and probably cost him a spot in Canton.

Helping a Giant Cause

Former NFL player George Martin did his part to assist forgotten 9/11 victims—one mile at a time

Favorite road trips of my career:

1. USO trip to Afghanistan, 2008. Hanging with troops. Hearing stories of firefights with the Taliban.

2. Bus trip across America with John Madden, 1990. Madden unplugged. Madden without the exclamation points.

3. Olympics in South Korea, 1988. Getting the Ben Johnson steroid scandal story for Newsday *with the help of an intrepid interpreter.*

4. Walking across 17 miles of Tennessee backroads with George Martin to help forgotten 9/11 victims for HBO, 2007. Keep reading.

"Ladies and gentleman," the Northwest flight attendant intoned last Wednesday evening, "our scheduled flight time from New York to Memphis today is two hours and 39 minutes. And if you're one of our valued WorldPerks members, you'll be credited with 986 miles for this flight."

I think Wayne Huizenga looks like the biggest doormat in the NFL. "I'm not upset with Nick. I think Nick is great. I love Nick Saban," he said in Janaury 2007. You love Nick Saban? This man who committed to coach your team for five years, who convinced you to hire 23 assistant coaches (aggregate salary for the 19 regular assistants and four "grad-assistant" types: about $6.7 million per year, most in the league except for Washington), who preached commitment to his players and walked out after two measly years, who left your franchise in worse shape than when he took it over ... you love this man?

That's when it hit me: My God, George Martin has walked this. All of it.

You may remember Martin as a 14-year New York Giant, an athletic defensive end who had a few moments of fame, including his sack of John Elway just before halftime of Super Bowl XXI; the safety started the G-men on a run of 26 unanswered points that opened the door to a 39–20 win. Martin is doing something slightly more important now.

I'm taking a detour from the games and the stars to start the column this week with a message from the real world, way out in rural west Tennessee.

Martin began walking from New York to San Francisco in September, and on Thursday, with me and an HBO crew in tow (for a profile on *Inside the NFL*), he walked the 1,000th mile of his trip just outside the little town of Bruceton, Tenn. I kept up with him for all of the day's 18 miles. And let me tell you, the man can walk.

Martin is walking to raise money and awareness for the mental and physical health problems that first-responders to the terrorist attacks at Ground Zero have suffered. Martin has raised $1.5 million of his $10 million goal; matching donors at three New York–area hospitals will boost the count to $3 million. Approximately 40,000 firefighters, police, EMS and volunteers have been affected by the inhalation of toxic con-

In California it is against the law for an adult to smoke in a car when a minor is a passenger. I remember the days when my parents smoked during dinner.

taminants from the pulverized buildings—and have contracted lung disease and even cancer—because most worked without protective masks. Even worse, some of those workers don't have health insurance, and a majority have inadequate health insurance to deal with the onslaught of new treatments they must use to stave off disease. At least eight first-responder deaths, including one of a nun, have been directly connected to Ground Zero poisoning.

"Have you watched film of that day?" Martin asked when we met on this morning. "Watch the scenes of all the people running from the site. Thousands of them. Then watch the people who are actually running *toward* the site, and watch the firefighters running into the buildings.

"It astounds me. It's so counterintuitive. But have we forgotten the events of that horrible day? Have we grown tired of the aftermath? If so, shame on us. When the first fatality came, it barely caused a whimper in the media. But I was touched deeply."

He had to do something. But what? Run a golf tournament to raise money for the second wave of 9/11 victims? A banquet?

I covered Martin late in his Giants career. The lithe defensive end was 32 when I met him, and the most mature man in the locker room. Some

From 10-27-08:
I think San Diego
will win
the AFC West.

*The Chargers, 3–5
after a bad loss
to New Orleans in
London, won five of
their last eight
to catch Denver and
win a tiebreaker
for the division.*

young teammates called him Pops. He was the cool head. Bill Parcells always thought if he coached one player who was going to save the world, it would be Martin. He started to, with the Giants, partnering with Fairleigh Dickinson University to get players to earn the degrees they never did at their original colleges; 16 teammates completed their schoolwork because of that program. The son of a South Carolina sharecropper, Martin lived the first 12 years of his life with a heavy sense of wanderlust tied to a 25-acre plot of ground; the family later moved to California, and he was a basketball and football player at Oregon before getting drafted by the Giants in 1975.

"I was an impressionable kid," he said. "I grew up in the time of the Kennedys. And I was really struck by two things they said. President Kennedy said, 'Ask not what your country can do for you. Ask what you can do for your country.' Bobby said, 'Some men see things as they are and say why? I dream of things that never were and say why not.' I met people, healthy people in their 40s and 50s, who can't walk up stairs anymore, who have to decide whether to spend the money they have on medicine or food, but sometimes not both. If I didn't do something to help this issue, then I wasn't the man I thought I was."

These people need money, Martin thought,

and not just $200,000. They need big money. He thought, 'I've got do something big' and then, 'This country needs to be reminded of the suffering of these heroes, and we've got to urge those in government to not forget them.'

So he took a leave from his job as a vice president at AXA Equitable in New York to walk 3,300 miles—from the George Washington Bridge to the Golden Gate Bridge, via the southern route because he'd be walking in the fall and winter. He decided he would do every interview, talk to everyone he met along the way about the issue, and stop at schools to spread the word. In essence, he set out to do something Kennedyesque.

Which brings us to Tennessee last Thursday. We started in Camden, in Benton County, on state highway 641 south just outside the Faith Christian Fellowship Church, on day 56 of his walk. (He has taken some days off for personal events, like his son's wedding.)

There was nothing momentous about our walk. We just walked, the two of us, and talked. "If I wrote a book about this," he said, "I'd have a chapter called 'Road Kill.' I've seen it all out here. Deer, possum, armadillo, snakes, squirrel, skunk. In Virginia, we were walking and all of a sudden out of the brush ahead of us comes this giant thing. It just wanders into the middle of

I liked this follow-up from Dillon: "It's not like I'm going to miss $5,000. I mean, $5,000. Oooooh."

the road. We get close enough to see it, and it's a hog. A 400-, 450-pound hog. Traffic stops. An 18-wheeler has to brake to stop from hitting it. The thing just sniffs the air for a while, doesn't smell anything like food, and goes back where it came from."

That was the conversation much of the day. Anything goes. Ten times he found some reason to come back to the cause. "The people have been amazing," he said. "The heartland is amazing. I'm walking one day, and an 18-wheeler stops and pulls over and the drivers leans out and says, 'You're George Martin.' I said, 'Yes I am, sir.' He says, 'I heard about what you're doing. Do you take donations?' And he gives me one right there. A couple of days ago, a pickup pulls over and the guy gets out, tells me how proud he is of what I'm doing and gives me $20. A while later, the same guy comes back—I guess he was ashamed of his original donation—and gives me $100 more. These people understand sacrifice, and they don't forget what makes this country great."

This is how much we walk: A reporter from a paper in Benton County pulls over on the side of the road a mile into the morning's walk, just after we turn onto U.S. 70, and asks Martin what he's doing. That afternoon, around 4, a reporter

Giving advice at a fantasy-football appearance in Red Wing, Minn., in August 2003, I uttered: "If you can't get one of the stud quarterbacks—Warner, Manning, Garcia, Favre, Gannon—then solve your running back and receiver needs in the first two or three rounds, then pick Danny Wuerffel." Said one fan in the audience: "You're smoking crack!"

from the next county's paper, in Carroll County, is waiting by the side of the road where another impromptu interview happens.

He talks about the impact of Bill Parcells a lot. "Every day I think about him, and about the lessons he taught me about so many things," Martin said. "Sometimes I'll be out here on the road and he'll call me. The other day he called and said, 'Hey Martin, you gotta get out of Tennessee! Winter's coming.' Bill's been great. He's the one who made the donation that got us over $1 million."

Parcells gave $10,000. Jim Fassel and Mark Bavaro have also given.

At one point on this 41°, raw, slate-gray day, Martin and I walk for at least four miles without seeing any man-made structures. We're walking through the woods, on a ribbon of asphalt. For an hour. And Martin loves it. "I haven't regretted the decision once. Not one time," he said. "I really consider it a blessing." And his health is good. It's amazing, but he has no strains, no sore back, nothing.

Martin travels with a medical technician to make sure that he's properly hydrated, a former New York City cop who walks with him and provides security, and an advance man to help with publicity and the scouting of the routes. On this day, Lee Reeves, the advance man, has arranged

I'm used to paying all kinds of taxes, but the tariffs in Houston in July 2002 beat all. A 54-cent phone call was taxed two cents because the Texas Legislature had put a 3.6% surcharge on all hotel phone calls. My Hyatt room was $215. The 6% state occupancy tax was $12.90, the 7% city occupancy tax $15.05, the 2% county occupancy tax $4.30, and the "sport occupancy" tax another $4.30. That, my desk clerk said, was to help pay for Minute Maid and Reliant stadiums. Glad to do my share, but an extra $36.57? Just for the privilege of staying in downtown Houston for 16 hours?

Age when Chuck Noll took the Steelers head coaching job in 1969: 37.
Age when Bill Cowher took the Steelers head coaching job in 1992: 34.
Age when Mike Tomlin took the Steelers head coaching job in 2007: 34.

for Martin to meet the police, fire and EMS workers in Bruceton (pop. 1,554), a railroad burg on the Big Sandy River, then to speak an impromptu school assembly at the K-12 school in town.

The school principal has downloaded Martin's theme song, *Walk a Mile in My Shoes*, and it's playing when he walks into the gym. When Martin takes the mike, you can tell he's done this before. He tells the kids that people have called him a hero, but he never saved anyone's life or taught classes how to read. Those are the heroes, he tells the kids.

And he has the kids give ovations to the police and fire and EMS workers, and another one to the teachers. The kids are rapt. And he tells them why he's making the walk, to help people like the ones who protect them every day.

Then he takes the police, fire and EMS folks out to lunch at a Mexican place. He's in no hurry. The mayor comes by to say hello. By 2:15, he's stretching again, then back on the road, where he sees an Amish family clip-clop by in their horse-and-buggy. "I didn't know there were Amish people here," he said. "You find out a lot you didn't know by taking this walk."

Late in the afternoon we pass a little ranch home, well-kept, with a pond in the front yard and a swing set on the side of the house. Martin stops on the side of the road and motions to the house. "See, something like this, it's beautiful," he said. "I've seen places like this a thousand times on this trip, but never one exactly like this. It's all new to me. I love it."

Martin is looking for a hotel sponsor to house his small crew along the way. He's looking for a gas sponsor for his two support vehicles. I asked Martin how the people who read this column could help his cause.

"People are in awe of the feat, of someone walking from New York to California," he said. "But that doesn't help us achieve our objective. Tell people to go to ajourneyfor911.info and please help the people who put their lives on the line for us—and are paying so dearly for it now."

'Tis the season.

If you believe in what Martin is doing, or if you love where you live, or both, ajourneyfor911. info should be your first stop today. Click on the donate bar. One man can make a difference. And you can help him prove it.

You contributed! You came through! You helped Martin with some $300,000 worth of coin. Martin will never forget your generosity. I'll never forget the walk.

At one point the same lawyer represented Barry Switzer, Jerry Jones and Larry Lacewell of the Cowboys. The lawyer's name was Larry Derryberry. They once dined together. At the table: Barry, Jerry, Larry and Larry Derryberry.

Greats of the Game

My Top 100 Players Of Today

Youth gets the edge, though my top three are QBs who've been dominant for some time now

I can stop many of the arguments you'll start here with one caveat: This list is quite a bit about the future. With a few notable exceptions—here's a couple: two alltime greats who are seemingly ageless, Brett Favre and Ray Lewis, make the list—my Top 100 is very heavy on youth and light on age, because I want this list to look good a year or two down the road.

Basically, I asked myself: If I'm building a team for a three- or five-year window, whom would I choose? And this is the order I came up with.

1. PEYTON MANNING, *QB, Colts*
The Interception Heard 'Round the World won't
dissuade me from keeping Manning at the top.

2. TOM BRADY, *QB, Patriots*
One MVP, three Super Bowl crowns ... and he'll
be healthier this year after '09 knee-rehabbing.

3. DREW BREES, *QB, Saints*
Two straight years for the ages help him
leapfrog all but the best two players in football.

4. DARRELLE REVIS, *CB, Jets*
Moves from 36th last year to No. 4 because he
quite simply is the best non-QB in the game.

5. BEN ROETHLISBERGER, *QB, Steelers*
Despite his troubles there's no indication he
won't be as good as ever come October.

6. LARRY FITZGERALD, *WR, Cardinals*
Numbers are bound to decline with Kurt Warner
gone, but he's still the most dangerous WR.

7. DeMARCUS WARE, *LB, Cowboys*
Name the last guy who had Ware's 2008 year:
20 sacks, 20 pressures. Great '09 too.

8. JARED ALLEN, *DE, Vikings*
Had one of the best games I've seen a defensive
player play in '09 at home against Green Bay.

9. MARIO WILLIAMS, *DE, Texans*
We laughed about the pick on draft day. Now
we see what Charley Casserly was doing.

10. ED REED, *FS, Ravens*
Seems to be hobbling toward Canton, but is still
the NFL's most dangerous ball hawking safety.

Whoa! Darrelle Revis at No. 4?
Last January I watched Philip Rivers systematically avoid Revis in the Chargers' playoff loss to the Jets. (Jets win. Rivers struggles. Hmmm. Wonder why.) Rivers completed a pass in the flat to LaDainian Tomlinson early, for a four-yard loss. That was the only ball a Revis-covered man caught all day. The guy is the most valuable non-QB in football.

15

There's a reason for the decline of Adrian Peterson. I still think he's a great player—the best running back in football. But the men in front of him were the leakiest in Peterson's three years, and Bryant McKinnie, especially, will have to rebound for Peterson to be the scary-good player he was in his first two years in the league.

11. PHILIP RIVERS, *QB, Chargers*
Touchdown passes in career years three through six: Rivers 105, Roethlisberger 93.

12. AARON RODGERS, *QB, Packers*
He didn't make Green Bay forget about Favre, but no one frets about the passing game.

13. CHARLES WOODSON, *CB, Packers*
It took a decade for him to dominate the way he did in college. For the Pack, it was worth the wait.

14. JOE THOMAS, *T, Browns*
He can maul, or he can play as athletically as any left tackle in the game.

15. ADRIAN PETERSON, *RB, Vikings*
Vike offensive line's failings pushed him back to mortal status in '09, with 4.4 yards per carry.

16. CHRIS JOHNSON, *RB, Titans*
Debated ranking him higher than Peterson. Concluded one scintillating year doesn't justify it.

17. ANDRE JOHNSON, *WR, Texans*
The best combination of physical receiver and deep threat in the league right now.

18. LaMARR WOODLEY, *LB, Steelers*
Dick LeBeau thinks he could be the best rush/pass-drop/run-stopping linebacker he's ever had.

19. PATRICK WILLIS, *LB, 49ers*
The best of the young crop of playmaking, field-roving middle linebackers.

20. NNAMDI ASOMUGHA, *CB, Raiders*
He's a younger, more durable cover-cornerback version of Champ Bailey.

21. JAHRI EVANS, *G, Saints*
Club rewarded league's best guard with contract making him a Saint for life in off-season.

22. JAMES HARRISON, *LB, Steelers*
The biggest defensive impact player of '08 made the greatest Super Bowl pick ever versus the Cards.

23. DWIGHT FREENEY, *DE, Colts*
Speed rusher should produce more pressure with Colts blitzing more in 2010.

24. TERRELL SUGGS, *DE/LB, Ravens*
Rushes, drops in coverage as well as any defender; plays all over the map.

25. KEVIN WILLIAMS, *DT, Vikings*
As lithe a 300-pound player as there has been in NFL history, but StarCaps suspension looms.

26. ROBERT MATHIS, *DE, Colts*
The more I talk to smart people, the more I've concluded Mathis is 95% the player Freeney is.

27. JUSTIN TUCK, *DE, Giants*
There's no more versatile defensive lineman today. Coming back from a shoulder injury.

28. HALOTI NGATA, *DT, Ravens*
Didn't have the dominating year in '09 he should have had, but he will this year. He wants to be paid.

29. TONY ROMO, *QB, Cowboys*
Gut feeling: This is the year people stop saying he's a crummy player in January.

30. RYAN CLADY, *T, Broncos*
Had a tremendous rookie year in '08; half a sack allowed, three penalties taken.

23

Dwight Freeney and Robert Mathis get the love they deserve. When you look at the stats, Freeney and Mathis are a lot closer in production than you'd ever think. After watching them for years, I honestly can say I think I've seen roughly the same numbers of big plays out of both. Thus the close call, and the placement of both in the top 30.

34

You want the next face of the NFL? It's Cortland Finnegan. Women swoon over him. He's engaging. He cares about the world. When addressing strangers, he uses *Mister* and *Ms.* He's reverent about the NFL, thrilled to be in it. He hits like a little Ronnie Lott. He covers like a glove. He's grateful for everything from the shoes on his feet to the free hats and shirts that NFL guys get thrown at them. He's going to be one of the best corners in the league for a long time.

31. NICK MANGOLD, *C, Jets*
A brawler. Mickey Rourke will play him in *The Life Story of Nick Mangold.*

32. MATT RYAN, *QB, Falcons*
Fell to earth a bit in his second year, but I see him as a top 10 QB, or better, for the next decade.

33. VINCE WILFORK, *NT, Patriots*
At 6' 2", 325 pounds, he's a superb space-eater in the classic 3–4 nosetackle mode.

34. CORTLAND FINNEGAN, *CB, Titans*
I called him the chippy little Hines Ward of corners. He loved it. It's what he is.

35. SIDNEY RICE, *WR, Vikings*
It took Brett Favre walking into the locker room to bring the best out of a great wideout.

36. BRANDON MARSHALL, *WR, Dolphins*
Now that he's gotten paid, this ball magnet has to be on his best behavior in Miami.

37. ELI MANNING, *QB, Giants*
A superhero in 2007, and the unquestioned leader of a young cadre of offensive skill players.

38. CALVIN JOHNSON, *WR, Lions*
He should emerge in the same class as Fitzgerald if his QB can be consistent and get him 90 balls.

39. DeANGELO WILLIAMS, *RB, Panthers*
In four years, he's shown both speed and power, at 5.1 yards a pop. Can't do much better than that.

40. WES WELKER, *WR, Patriots*
Will miss part of 2010 after knee surgery, but no WR has more catches in the last three years.

41. JAKE LONG, *T, Dolphins*
He lived up to the hype of the first overall pick with great drive blocking in the '08 season.

42. MATT SCHAUB, *QB, Texans*
He still needs to win a Big One, but he threw for 270 yards more than any QB in football last year.

43. DALLAS CLARK, *TE, Colts*
Bill Polian actually said this with a straight face last year: Clark was his team's MVP.

44. JULIUS PEPPERS, *DE, Bears*
I happen to think a truly great defensive end should average more than 10 sacks a year.

45. DARNELL DOCKETT, *DT, Cardinals*
He'll have to take on a bigger role this season with four Arizona defensive defections.

46. ANTHONY SPENCER, *LB, Cowboys*
He and D-Ware were my two all-pro OLBs in '09. This year he'll convince the rest of the league.

47. JOE FLACCO, *QB, Ravens*
I left him off my list last year, a glaring omission. I expect he'll make me pay for a long time.

48. JOSH CRIBBS, *RB/WR/Ret/Special Teams, Browns*
There is no dispute: He's the best all-around special teamer in football.

49. DeSEAN JACKSON, *WR/Ret, Eagles*
Every year it seems there's a new scariest WR-returner in the league. This year, it's Jackson.

50. VINCENT JACKSON, *WR, Chargers*
How dare I put Jackson this high! I dare because I watched him sky over corners all year long.

44

Enough with the Julius Peppers hype machine. How can you not like Peppers as a player? He never complains. But the key word there is *like*, not *love*. How many times have you watched a Carolina game and come away thinking that Peppers was the best player on the field today? I never did. I think the same will be the case in Chicago, where he landed as a rich free agent. There's nothing bad about that. He's a good-to-very-good NFL defensive end. But he was supposed to be the next Reggie White, and what he has been is 15% better than Justin Smith.

52

Brett Favre and Ray Lewis are going to play till they're 65, so I give up putting them down. This should be a list for the present *and* the future. I've always thought I'd like the list to stand up for the next two or three years at least. But Favre (33–7 TD–pick ratio) and Ravens-leading tackler Ray Lewis were so good last season in what should been a year well past their primes that I've changed my mind. If they show no sign of retiring, or slowing down, they make the list.

51. STEVEN JACKSON, *RB, Rams*
Can he survive long enough to still be good when the Rams get good? My guess: no.

52. BRETT FAVRE, *QB, Vikings*
This list considers the future and the present. But you tell me when age slows this man.

53. RAY LEWIS, *LB, Ravens*
See number 52. Even at 35 years old he's still an age-defying tackling machine.

54. STEVE HUTCHINSON, *G, Vikings*
Play dropped in '09 with shoulder injury, but still the most technically sound lineman in football.

55. JABARI GREER, *CB, Saints*
Went from an athlete playing corner to superb all-around corner in Saints' Super Bowl run.

56. SHANE LECHLER, *P, Raiders*
In '09 became the first punter in the modern era to average 50 yards (51.1 if you want to be exact).

57. CHRIS SNEE, *G, Giants*
The best argument for nepotism in NFL history; a burly enforcer with great technique.

58. JASON WITTEN, *TE, Cowboys*
Numbers don't matter as much for Witten, the best blocking-receiving TE in Dallas history.

59. MAURICE JONES-DREW, *RB, Jaguars*
Hope he has the durability of a bigger man. One of the 10 most enjoyable players to watch.

60. DAVID STEWART, *T, Titans*
Eclipsed teammate and shadow-caster Michael Roos in play in 2009.

61. CHAD GREENWAY, *LB, Vikings*
Versatile playmaker who is taking over more
and more of a leader role on a changing D.

62. REGGIE WAYNE, *WR, Colts*
Could Marvin Harrison and Wayne both catch
1,000 balls and both struggle to make the Hall?

63. ELVIS DUMERVIL, *LB, Broncos*
The Broncos made the made right call, moving
him from a small DE to rush OLB in 2009.

64. CARL NICKS, *G, Saints*
Yes, teammate Jahri Evans is the best guard in
football. But Nicks is very close.

65. CULLEN JENKINS, *DL, Packers*
Versatile run and pass-rush defender who keys so
much of what Pack does to make their scheme go.

66. DONOVAN McNABB, *QB, Redskins*
Still seems very strange to write *Redskins*
after his name. Should lift them to .500.

67. MIKE SCIFRES, *P, Chargers*
Belongs here because of the greatest playoff
game a punter ever had (six punts, 51.7 net).

68. MICHAEL GRIFFIN, *FS, Titans*
Shows an Ed Reed–type presence in Titans'
back end, with great instinct for the ball.

69. D'BRICKASHAW FERGUSON, *T, Jets*
Slow starter in his career. Not the brute strength
of a Joe Thomas, but solid all-around protector.

70. JUSTIN SMITH, *DE, 49ers*
Led team with 78 QB pressures and 52 hits in '09.
Proves you don't have to get sacks to be effective.

70

Justin Smith has finally won me over. 49ers coach Mike Singletary speaks in reverential tones about Smith, a DE who doesn't sack the quarterback much but buzzes around his head all the time. For years I thought the sack was ultraimportant in judging the end position, and finishing is obviously vital in rushing the QB. But Smith's exterior pressure was so important in helping the Niners climb the defensive charts in '09 so I've gained profound respect for his game-affecting rush.

75

Shonn Greene is on this list? Really? When I watched the Jets last year, especially in the playoff game against San Diego, I thought Greene might be the next great NFL back. So after Thomas Jones was allowed to leave in free agency, I became convinced Greene will have every chance in the world to contend for a rushing title. He's got the quickness and a bit of between-the-tackles power you need to be able to run inside and outside.

71. LEON HALL, *CB, Bengals*
Turned into a true shutdown corner in '09, helping Bengals' front play better than it was.

72. GREG JENNINGS, *WR, Packers*
A little smurfy at 5' 11", but all that matters is he gets open like few receivers in football.

73. TRENT COLE, *DE, Eagles*
Had the quietest 12½-sack season in NFL history. This is the guy the Eagles can't play without on D.

74. JAY CUTLER, *QB, Bears*
He'll prove he's not an interception machine with Mike Martz choreographing the Chicago O.

75. SHONN GREENE, *RB, Jets*
Just watch: The Jets' faith in him will be rewarded this year, when he rushes for 1,400 yards.

76. BOBBIE WILLIAMS, *G, Bengals*
Ask Cedric Benson why his career got revived—it's much because Williams paved some big holes.

77. DARREN SPROLES, *RB/Ret, Chargers*
Norv Turner's got to find a way to give him 275 touches this year. I said the same thing last year.

78. AUBRAYO FRANKLIN, *DT, 49ers*
Probably the most unknown player on this list—but just watch him push the pile. A monster.

79. CLAY MATTHEWS, *LB, Packers*
Watch his tour de force against Steelers last November to see what a game changer he is.

80. LOGAN MANKINS, *G, Patriots*
Excellent technician, solid as a rock. Might be best Pats guard since John Hannah.

81. RANDY MOSS, *WR, Patriots*
Love Moss, debated putting him much higher.
Just not sure how long he can stay healthy.

82. ALBERT HAYNESWORTH, *DT, Redskins*
When he's a team guy, he's a top 15 player. He
just doesn't play like that for long stretches.

83. STEPHEN GOSTKOWSKI, *K, Patriots*
It's absurd to think "Adam who?" But this guy
might make Pats fans do it.

84. DOMINIQUE RODGERS-CROMARTIE, *CB, Cardinals*
Finally Arizona has a cornerback who can
shut down speedy wideouts.

85. NICK BARNETT, *LB, Packers*
Sideline-to-sideline playmaker who really raised
his game last year

86. TONY GONZALEZ, *TE, Falcons*
Falls in the Favre-Ray Lewis category, players who
should be declining but aren't. Still a threat

87. DeMECO RYANS, *LB, Texans*
Tackling machine who plays bigger than he is.
Every defense needs a rangy MLB like him.

88. BARRETT RUUD, *LB, Bucs*
One of the reasons why Derrick Brooks was cut in
'09 was to make Ruud the Bucs' defensive boss.

89. LANCE BRIGGS, *LB, Bears*
I'd like to see more big plays, but he's an
always-around-the-ball tackling machine.

90. ASANTE SAMUEL, *CB, Eagles*
Most would rate him higher, but he needs to be
more physical to move up on my food chain.

86

**We need to start
polishing a bust
for Tony
Gonzalez for
Canton.** Gonzalez
is 34. He has
more catches
than any tight end
in NFL history.
In his first
10 years in
the league, he
averaged 72.1
catches a year.
In his last three
years, at ages 31,
32 and 33, he has
averaged 92.7
catches. Imagine
being significantly
more productive in
your 30s than your
20s in such a
debilitating game.
Heck of a player.

97

Roddy White will be the greatest receiver in Falcons history by 2013. That's like saying Peter King's the best sportswriter in the history of Enfield, Conn. In other words, not much competition. Wallace Francis? Andre Rison? Terance Mathis? White has the discipline and physical tools, and he has the young, strong-armed, smart, accurate quarterback in Matt Ryan. When we look back on White's career we just might say the same thing about him that we'll say about Marvin Harrison. Very good player . . . and very lucky that his team drafted a great quarterback to get him the ball.

91. ANTONIO GATES, *TE, Chargers*
Too many nagging injuries to be considered better than tough-guy Jason Witten.

92. ADRIAN WILSON, *S, Cardinals*
He's the Cards' muscle and will be even better with ball hawking Kerry Rhodes alongside him.

93. SANTONIO HOLMES, *WR, Jets*
Rex Ryan could never stop him when coaching the Ravens, so he pilfered him for a fifth-rounder.

94. JON BEASON, *LB, Panthers*
Middle 'backers today need to be rangy and hit brutally, and Beason is classic at both.

95. SHAUN PHILLIPS, *LB, Chargers*
This playmaker broke through for 35½ sacks, QB pressures and tackles for loss in '08.

96. JORDAN GROSS, *T, Panthers*
Amazingly true: He has switched from right to left to right to left to right to left tackle as a pro.

97. RODDY WHITE, *WR, Falcons*
An immature guy who got whipped into top-receiver shape by WR coach Terry Robiskie.

98. TROY POLAMALU, *SS, Steelers*
Pains me to drop a truly great player this low, but I'm not sure he's a long-termer with his knees.

99. CHAMP BAILEY, *CB, Broncos*
I worry about his age (32) and whether he's really Champ Bailey anymore.

100. KRIS JENKINS, *DT, Jets*
For the first half of 2008 he was the defensive player of the year. Needs to stay healthy.

MMQB Classic February 4, 2002

The Sincerest Form of Flattery

Bill Belichick's Patriots emerged from their first Super Bowl victory with the look of a model franchise

There was something about the Patriots' Super Bowl upset of the two-touchdown-favored Rams nine seasons ago. New England wasn't that good, and this drive led by some nobody named Tom Brady might have just been a fluky drive at the end of a game, and . . . well, it was obvious afterward that the football world didn't think it was seeing the start of a great run by Bill Belichick's Patriots. I'm not saying I saw it either, but what I did see was a really smart guy coaching a team the right way.

It was shortly after 1 o'clock on Monday morning in New Orleans, on the mezzanine level of the New England Patriots' grand old team hotel, the Fairmont. Bill Belichick was in a strange little conga line outside the ballroom barely holding the rollicking team party, waiting for two Louisiana state

The next 10 on my list of the greatest active players:

101. Alex Mack, *C, Browns*

102. Michael Oher, *T, Ravens*

103. Jamaal Charles, *RB, Chiefs*

104. Jerod Mayo, *LB, Patriots*

105 Tony Brown, *DT, Titans*

106. Ryan Harris, *T, Broncos*

107. Devin Hester, *WR/KR, Bears*

108. Carson Palmer, *QB, Bengals*

109. Pierre Thomas, *RB, Saints*

110. Willie Colon, *T, Steelers*

I think Ray Lewis is going to be happy with his standing on this list. The last time I did a ranking of active players, in 2007, and had Lewis at No. 86, he went quasi-bonkers on me at training camp. In a friendly way—I think. "What's your *criteria*!" I said this list was about the present and future, and I doubted that, at 32, he had three or four prime years left. So what did he do? He went out and had a great 2008 and '09. I can just hear Ray Lewis now. "King! How do you like me now!?"

police officers to organize the route into the party. He carried a drained Corona bottle in one hand. He wore a Super Bowl hat slightly askew on his head and a light brown suit. His wife, Deb, high-school daughter, Amanda, his boyhood buddy Mark Fredland and close aide Berj Najarian were along for what, in a moment, was going to a bumpy ride.

"You realize," I said to the Super Bowl–winning coach, "that you've probably just changed how people are going to build teams now. You bring in 17 schmoes and win the Super Bowl. . . . "

Belichick smiled. By the 17 low-cost free agents, I meant the Larry Izzos and Terrell Buckleys and Mike Comptons and Otis Smiths and Mike Vrabels, veteran middle-of-the-roster guys, each of whom cost less than $700,000 to sign during last year's free-agent rummage sale. And he recalled what his old personnel man from the Cleveland days had told him after the Wal-Mart spree that Belichick and his underrated director of player personnel, Scott Pioli, went on last spring. "Mike Lombardi [now an Oakland scout] called me after we signed all those guys," Belichick said, "and he told me what a good job he thought we'd done. He told me, 'You'll be successful and other teams are gonna look at this and build teams like you did.' "

It didn't look that way early. I saw Michael Strahan on Sunday morning and he told me he remembered going to scrimmage the Patriots in August with his Giants. "They were terrible, an awful football team," he said. Then they were at 0–2, and at 1–3, coming off a 20-point loss at Miami. No one was thinking of modeling anything after these Patriots then, except maybe how to have rumors start about the coach getting fired after two bad years. "Super Bowl?" Belichick said, a stunned look on his face. "Are you kidding me? What's that thing Jim Mora said when the Colts had lost a bunch in a row?"

I said, "'Playoffs? *Playoffs?* We're just trying to win a game!'"

"Yeah," Belichick said. "My whole thing with this team was, 'Let's just get better. Let's just get a little better every day.' And, you know, of all the teams I've ever been around, these guys try so hard. They really try to do what you tell them."

I told him I was amazed, as the pool reporter at Patriots' practices during the week, that not once in three afternoons of working his team did he raise his voice. I found that amazing. A guy as acerbic and pointed and blunt as Belichick can be, going through five hours and 56 minutes of football practice (I'm anal; I counted) without being loud. A Bill Parcells underling not being bellicose? Not even close. Not to go mystic or anything, but I'm telling you: Belichick and this team

"Would you have any problem playing in a colder climate, like a Minnesota?"

—Reporter's question to Georgia Tech wide receiver Calvin Johnson at the 2007 scouting combine. The Vikings have played in a dome since 1982.

were at one. They knew what he wanted. They knew how to give it to him.

"Well," Belichick said, "don't let that kid you. We've had some sessions with those guys, some real tough sessions. But all you can ask of players is to work hard and to try to get better every day."

It's boring. It's not the Greatest Show on Turf. It also wins. That's why, as Lombardi says, this will be copied. Oh, this most definitely will be copied.

Now it was time for the Belichick party to crash the party. These cops were serious. As we came around a bend, there were three partyers on a band of hotel pay phones. For no apparent reason—they weren't in the way—the cops literally moved them forcefully away from the pay phones while the people were still using them; one of the dislodged phones just clattered against the wall. "What are you *do*—?" was all one party-dressed woman said before being moved.

Patriots coming through. Make way.

Everyone's going to wonder what kind of fluke this was. No fluke. Mike Martz was right coming in: This is a supremely well-coached team with enough talent. You scoff at that? I don't. Because this is the key to life in the NFL today: Every team has enough talent. It's how the talent is coached and orchestrated, and how the coaches make the talent 10% better than it would be somewhere

United says it serves brewed Starbucks on its flights, and the aroma wafting from the galleys certainly smells good. But if anything, it's faux Starbucks, mild and Chase-and-Sanbornish. My guess is they run too much water through the coffee, rendering it weak and ineffective, because anyone who calls that coffee also must think it is fair for the Tampa Bay Rays to be in the AL East.

else. Coaching in the NFL means more than in any other sport, ever.

Football is a succession of plays. If all teams are close in talent, doesn't it make sense that the people who give you the edge in a few plays every game make up the better team? On Friday, Belichick mentioned to offensive coordinator Charlie Weis that a red-zone pass play with David Patten—one of the bargain-basement guys—doing an out route at the goal line might be improved to an out-up-and-go. The thinking, from Belichick, the old tape-head, was that lots of video had shown that St. Louis cornerback Dexter McCleon was prone to bite on the out near the goal line. So Belichick wanted to have Patten sell the out, then fly to the corner of the end zone. They never ran it in practice last week, simply telling Tom Brady and Patten of the switch on Saturday morning. Of course the play happened in the game. Of course McCleon bit. And of course Brady threw it perfectly to Patten for the touchdown.

Vrabel's careening rush on Kurt Warner, which forced the Ty Law pick that gave New England an early 7–3 lead, was another example of unfamous players making Super Bowl–turning plays. When I asked Vrabel, the strongside 'backer, about the Pats' signings, he smiled. "The has-beens and never-will-be's," he said after the game. "That's us. We

Aboard a crowded 8:11 New Jersey Transit train from Upper Montclair to Penn Station in January 2007, I heard the clip-clip-snip-clip-snip sound of a woman cutting her fingernails with a nail clipper, then flicking them from her lap to the floor. I looked at the guy next to me, and we raised eyebrows; "Dare you to say something," I said. He just shook his head. So this is permitted in the human race now? The clipping of nails, and disposing of them on the floor? Who was it, in some famous movie, who said, "I weep for the future?" I echo that.

I think Gunther Cunningham's ripping of the San Diego press corps because they weren't giving him enough stuff to read about the Chargers on the Internet is one of the wackiest things I've ever read. "You can't get any good information out of San Diego," Cunningham, then coach of the Kansas City Chiefs, said in October 1999. "When you have a media outlet like San Diego, you might as well go to Tijuana. San Diego stinks." I love it! Coach rips the media because they won't spy for him. It's a beautiful dotcom society we live in.

proved here that football's the ultimate team game."

Once at the party, Belichick accepted hugs from Patriots people and fans. I went to visit his dad. Steve Belichick is a peppy and talkative 83, and he got Bill into the coaching routine when the kid was eight or nine. Bill sort of helped Steve, then an assistant coach at the Naval Academy, break down opponents' game tapes on the projector at home in Annapolis, Md. This was a proud papa, but no more proud than he was before the Patriots won the Super Bowl.

"What did you tell your son after the game?" I asked Belichick the elder.

"I told him, 'You finally won one on your own,'" he said.

True. And the rest of the league was watching very, very closely.

The Patriots aren't done yet, though the window isn't very wide-open anymore, with the Jets and Dolphins catching up. I could see Belichick coaching there another five years and, with Brady at the helm, having a chance to win the Super Bowl every year. But the running game, receivers group and pass rushers all seem to be coming up short five years removed from the team's last title. Belichick's still a great coach, but the next couple of seasons will prove if he's as good a personnel man.

MMQB Classic November 13, 2000

Field Hockey Novella

I've seen some of the greatest pro and college games ever, but none compare to this high school thriller

I love high school sports. I remember once, a few years ago, being in San Diego to cover the Chargers' NFL draft the next day, and I had some time to kill, and I found a girls softball game in some suburb. I just plopped down on the bleachers and spent two glorious hours watching complete strangers play and coach and root. I don't know what it is—I think it's because they're kids (ours, oftentimes) trying so valiantly to do something that, at that moment, is the most important thing in the world to them. Because my two daughters played field hockey and softball, I began writing about it.

Now, I've gotten tons of criticism over the years from people who just want me to write about football. When I first started writing Monday Morning Quarterback, my editor said he wanted to see some of my personality in it. "This new thing, the Internet, is going to be different," he said. "When you write, people are going to want to know some-

On the night that Michael Phelps swam for his record eighth gold medal, the New York Giants were spending their final night at training camp at the University at Albany. Thirteen offensive linemen gathered around a big-screen plasma TV in a dorm room. Phelps dived in and lengthened the U.S. lead in the 4×100 medley relay. *"U-S-A! U-S-A!"* the linemen chanted. When the race was won, they all sang *God Bless America* at the top of their off-key lungs. Center Shaun O'Hara told me, "What a night. The coolest thing. Pretty patriotic. Pretty memorable."

thing about you and what your opinions and likes and dislikes are." So who doesn't like talking and writing about himself? Thus, personal stuff in my column was born. And game stories of big events in my kids' sporting lives came alive, like this game, which left me breathless.

I have been to nine World Series games. I have been to 16 Super Bowls, two Olympics and a Stanley Cup. I have been present for Dan Marino's last win, John Elway's biggest win, Bill Buckner's biggest miss, the Bills' 32-point playoff comeback, Michael Jordan's freshman-year national championship shot to beat Georgetown and Jim Valvano's Wolfpack's shocking Houston. But there is no sports event I will remember like a field hockey game played on a little field across from an elementary school in my hometown of Montclair, N.J., last week.

If you read this column, you know my autumnal team of choice is the Montclair High field hockey team, with my elder daughter, senior Laura King, on right wing. Field hockey is much like soccer, with 11 tireless, skirted girls per side on a field about the same size as a soccer pitch but with a much smaller goal, curved sticks and an orange plastic ball the size and density of a baseball.

Our season record of 16-2-1 earned MHS

When the Patriots released their Physically Unable to Perform list at the start of their 2008 training camp, the first three names on the alphabetized list were:
• BenJarvus Green-Ellis.
• Jarvis Green.
• Ellis Hobbs.
BenJarvus Green-Ellis, Jarvis Green, Ellis.

the host's role in the New Jersey Group IV Section I semifinal game against 12-4-1 Livingston. At breakfast that morning, Laura said: "I just can't believe this might be my last game." When Livingston scored midway through the second half, I feared Laura was right. Parents became frantic on the sidelines. We made so much noise that six New Jersey Transit railway workers, doing repair work on the commuter tracks just behind the west side of the field, stopped work to watch the game and yell encouragement. Our kids pressed. Finally, in the last minute of regulation, our all-world midfielder, Nicki Cozzolino, weaved through a throng of Lancers, centered the ball, and left wing Alexis Barbalinardo slapped a shot into the back of the cage. Thirty-two seconds left. Delirium. Momentum, us.

"What are the rules now?!" one of the railroad guys yelled.

"Overtime!" I yelled back. Now they'd play a 10-minute sudden-death OT, with seven players a side to stimulate offensive chances. Then another, if it was still 1–1. Then a round of five penalty strokes, just like soccer penalty kicks. Then another round of five. Then, gulp, sudden-death penalty strokes: The game ends when the first stroke beats a goalie.

Our field has small bleachers on the side of

Two things about BenJarvus Green-Ellis:

1) He might be the first person in NFL history with two first names, two last names and two colleges. He played two years at Indiana, transferred, then played two years at Ole Miss.

2) He might be the first player in college football history to lead one Division I school in rushing for two years, transfer, then lead another Division I school in rushing for two years. He had 938 and 794 yards at IU, sat out a season, then 999 and 1,137 at Mississippi.

In August 2006 Ben Dogra, the agent for safety Roy Williams, negotiated a rich contract extension for Williams with the Dallas Cowboys. In October 2008 Ben Dogra, the agent for wide receiver Roy Williams, negotiated a rich contract extension for Williams with the Dallas Cowboys. Dogra, Roy Williams and Roy Williams dined in St. Louis last fall. I'm not sure, but I think there's a good chance that Roy Williams picked up the check.

the field, stands that were packed at the start of the game. At the end of regulation most of the 200 people in attendance got off the bleachers and packed the sidelines. When the overtime began, you couldn't hear stick strike ball over all the screaming. We had a 2-on-1 midway through the overtime—Laura and linemate Erika Hamdan—and the Livingston goalie stoned them. Laura got tackled in the goal crease.

"Penalty shot! Penalty shot!" Railroad Guy yelled. The two refs conferred and green-carded the offending Lancer. The poor girl went to the sidelines and buried her head in the ground, crushed. Now we'd have a 7-on-6 edge for five minutes. No score. Momentum, Livingston. No score in the second OT, either. Now each team picked five girls to take alternating penalty strokes.

The pressure. The overwhelming pressure. Your entire season comes down to a goalie moving the right way or wrong way. Or which corner the shooter aims for.

Each team lined up behind the shooters, Montclair to the left, Livingston to the right. Every player intertwined hands with a teammate, holding hands so hard they thought fingers might get broken. Cool senior Natalie Serock, our ace stroker, had made two of four of these rare shots in her career, and she would shoot first. Her mother had to turn away. "I can't look," Rita Serock kept repeating.

Suddenly, silence. For two, three, four seconds. Natalie crouched, poised to take the shot. The ref blew his whistle. Natalie shot . . . and it thudded into the Livingston goalie's glove. Save! Livingston's shooter repeated everything Natalie had done—except she hit her shot perfectly. Score! Then we missed. They missed. Our Devon O'Neill, one of the steadiest, most reliable players you'll see on any field, went high right with her stroke. Score! Tie game! I hugged half of Montclair, and I would have bear-hugged Railroad Guy had he been next to me. Then they missed, we missed, they missed, we missed, they missed. Still tied.

Now a second round of strokes, with five different shooters. The pressure. Unrelenting. One of our fans, Jim Zarrilli, had bypass surgery a couple of years ago, and I looked over to see him pacing and holding his chest. The first nine shooters—five for us, four for them—all missed, with the goalies doing a tremendous clutch job. Now it was time for the 10th Livingston stroke. Silence. Dead silence. The girl shot to goalie Kaitlyn Robinson's right and beat her!

No! No!

"He built this team like the first little pig built his house."

—Bears radio voice Dan Hampton in 2000. The Hall of Fame defensive lineman evidently had little use for the personnel acumen of ex-Chicago coach Dave Wannstedt.

On a San Diego–bound United flight in 2003, the following announcement was made to us vermin in coach: "Ladies and gentlemen, we have lavatory facilities in both the forward and rear cabins of our aircraft. In order to maintain the integrity of both cabins we kindly ask that you use the facilities in your individual cabin on our flight today. Thank you very much." I always thought you maintained integrity by not cheating on a test, or by not committing adultery. I never knew you maintained integrity by using a certain bathroom in a long metal tube.

"Clang!" The ball hit the post and bounded harmlessly away. Momentum, us.

Sudden-death strokes now. Our best, then their best. For the game. Our best was Natalie. A long time ago, in fourth and fifth grade, my wife and I had coached Natalie in a Montclair girls' softball league. Most girls at that age are silly half of the time, but not Natalie. She was serious, and cool. We decided she'd be our pitcher, and I bet we lost three or four games with her, at most. She'd be 3-and-0 on a kid, the other team would be chanting for a walk, and she'd come back with three consecutive strikes. When times were tense, she was the best. And now, I silently begged for her to be the best once more. A third of our team couldn't watch now, their heads buried in teammates' shoulders. One of the tri-captains, Perri Hillsberg, told me later: "I was biting Alexis's shoulder. Literally biting her. I couldn't take the pressure."

Silence. The only sound came from a distance; a train whistle blew. Natalie reset herself. The ref blew his whistle. And on the 11th penalty stroke, after two fruitless rounds of strokes, after two fruitless overtimes, after a desperation goal saved a 60-minute heart-stopper, Natalie calmly flicked the ball just to the right of the goalie's pads into the back of the goal.

It was a blur after that; Livingston missing its shot; strangers hugging; parents crying; me jumping eight feet off the ground in a silly pirouette; the entire team burying Kaitlyn, the goalie, for saving the game; and Perri weeping on her father's shoulder and screaming: "I never want to go through that again!" And the poor Livingston kids. No one deserves that torture. They wept—the goalie sobbing uncontrollably—as the two sides shook hands, and a couple of our kids cried just seeing them. "I feel absolutely terrible for them," Laura said. "No one should have to lose that way."

As Natalie and her parents walked to their car, someone asked her what she was thinking when she lined up for that last penalty stroke.

"I was thinking, 'She hasn't seen my best shot yet,' " Natalie said.

Montclair fell out of the state playoffs three days later, losing at New Jersey's eighth-ranked team, Morris Knolls, 1–0. Valiant effort. Just result. The kids fought to the end, but the other team was better. As we hugged Laura after the game, she said, "We tried soooo hard." We knew. And Saturday, in a hastily scheduled makeup with archrival Northern Highlands, a team that MHS hadn't beaten since 1997, the girls shook off their disappointment and dominated, winning 2–0. We finished 17-3-1, and though one of

From 6-3-02: I think the next controversial blip on the NFL radar screen could be human grown hormone, which smart players are using because it won't come up as a positive in steroid or ephedra testing. HGH has a lot of the same harmful side effects of steroids, and people I know in the league say they're noticing more acceptance of HGH by players.

the greatest seasons of their lives was over, the girls swore they wouldn't cry.

Last week the Arizona Cardinals, who don't belong on the same field with the Redskins in talent, beat Washington 16–15 behind their emotional pepperpot of an interim head coach, Dave McGinnis. After the game, McGinnis gathered his team in the locker room, told them to be silent and rasped: "You hear that? That's one heart beating!" That's passion. Bobby Ross quit the Lions because he didn't have it, and he saw his players didn't. Rare are the great teams in football, or in any sport, that play businesslike and win big.

The hope for our kids, everywhere, is that they grow up to do something with passion, something they love, and that they learn the true meaning of teamwork. High school sports are a perfect place for that passion to develop. After the Livingston game last week, I asked Perri if she wanted to be one of the penalty-strokers, if she wanted a piece of the glory that would go along with making such a crucial shot. "I don't care if I've got one of those shots," she said with feeling. "I don't care if I'm in Kalamazoo. I just want us to win."

See how much kids can teach us?

I still get goose bumps remembering that day. I'm just an old cornball.

From 3-15-04: I think the Cowboys got a great deal in Drew Henson, whom they acquired from the Houston Texans for a third-round pick in the 2005 draft and then signed to a relatively modest contract (an eight-year deal, with the final four years voidable).

Ten Things I Think I Think

Turn the Card In . . . and Hurry

A pair of Patriots quarterbacks highlight my list of the 10 best draft choices since the 1970 merger

1. TOM BRADY, *QB, 2000, sixth round (199th overall),*
Patriots. Three Super Bowl victories in his first four
years as a starter in New England is good enough
to earn the top spot on this list, but the man was
drafted after Spergon Wynn (quarterback, Southwest Texas State, by the Browns). That's all you
need to know.

2. LARRY BROWN, *CB, 1991, 12th round (320th*
overall), Cowboys. I know what you're going to say—
Brown wasn't that good. You're right. But you tell
me another time the 320th overall pick in a draft
started without hurting a Super Bowl winner—
and won a Super Bowl MVP award.

3. MATT CASSEL, *QB, 2005, seventh round (225th over-*
all), Patriots. What I'd like to know is this: How did
then New England scouting VP Scott Pioli see a
starting NFL quarterback in a guy who had never
started a game in college? In some ways this success story is even more surprising than Brady's.

I think I cannot
believe that the
NFL didn't let
Peyton Manning
wear hightops in
September 2002,
to honor Johnny
Unitas. How
unfeeling.
Unconscionable.
Hey Park Avenue:
Your uniform is not
so sacred that
a player should be
kept from having
three extra inches
of black on his
ankles. There's a
time to be rigid,
and a time to
honor one of the
greatest players in
NFL history. There
are many good,
fan-appealing
things about the
NFL. But this
bit of coldness is
not one of them.

4. BRIAN SIPE, *QB, 1972, 13th round, (330th overall), Browns.* NFL Quiz: Name the sandy-haired quarterback, who later led a team to the Super Bowl as a head coach, who was chosen 163 spots ahead of Sipe in the draft? (Insert "Final Jeopardy" theme music here.) Answer: Jim Fassel.

5. JOE MONTANA, *QB, 1979, third round (82nd overall), 49ers.* Another little-known tidbit of NFL history: The quarterback that Bill Walsh wanted badly in this draft—so much so that both he and quarterback coach Sam Wyche journeyed to a tiny campus in eastern Kentucky in the fortnight before the draft to interview him—was Phillip Martin Simms of Morehead State. The Giants, of course, beat San Francisco to him in the first round. Montana wasn't a bad consolation prize, winning four Super Bowls (and MVP honors three times).

6. JOE FIELDS, *C, 1975, 14th round (349th overall), Jets.* Anyone else from the 14th round start in the NFL for 12 years, lately? And make two Pro Bowls? And totally frustrate the vaunted Miami Dolphins defensive line?

7. ZACH THOMAS, *LB, 1996, fifth round (154th overall), Dolphins.* If Jimmy Johnson wasn't coaching the Cowboys then and had been out of football, Thomas might have gone undrafted. Who drafts 228-pound linebackers? All Thomas did was make seven Pro Bowls.

"Joe looked like a Swedish placekicker when we drafted him."

—San Francisco coach Bill Walsh in December 2006, looking back on his third-round selection of Joe Montana in 1979.

8. BO JACKSON, *RB, 1987, seventh round (183rd overall), Los Angeles Raiders.* You forgot this, didn't you? A year after the Tampa Bay Bucs picked him first overall and failed to sign him, Jackson signed a contract with the Kansas City Royals and began a baseball career. The Raiders took a flyer on him, and got him to play part-time at the end of baseball seasons by agreeing to pay him like a full-time back. His 221-yard Monday night performance at Seattle in his fifth NFL game is still one of the legendary performances by a running back ever. But Jackson lasted only four seasons because of a hip injury sustained against Cincinnati in the 1990 playoffs.

9. STEVE TASKER, *special teams player, 1985, ninth round (226th overall), Oilers.* This is easy. Tasker lasted 12 seasons in Buffalo after being waived in Houston, and there's little question he's the best special-teamer in NFL history.

10. RANDY MOSS, *WR, 1998, first round (21st overall), Vikings.* After 20 players had been selected, Minnesota coach Dennis Green did what everyone else had refused to do: play with fire. And he managed that fire well. Moss produced 90 touchdowns in seven seasons with the Vikings before flaming out and getting traded to Oakland. Jerry Jones later said passing on Moss was the biggest draft-day mistake he ever made. He's in good company. ●

"Big win, Eric," I said to Eric Mangini a little after 6 o'clock on Sept. 28, 2008, after the Jets pounded the Cardinals 56–35. "But it's not the biggest event of your day. You know what's bigger?" "Sure do," he said. "It's the season premiere of *Family Guy*." Bingo! In no particular order, Mangini is a big fan of *The Office, Curb Your Enthusiasm*, and *Extras*. Sense of humor: wry.

MMQB Classic March 2, 2009

Chris Canty's Foray into Free Agency

As one player's story showed, the ability to read and react is as critical off the football field as it is on it

Among the prospects in the 2002 NFL draft class were an Antwoine, an Antuan, an Antwaan, an Anton, an Antwon and an Antwan.

In the winter of 2009 I got the chance to follow the free-agent trail with agent Brad Blank, representing a player that a lot of football fans didn't know. Chris Canty was either going to get very rich or be very disappointed.

Chris Canty must be sick to his stomach. He was on a roller coaster all weekend.

There is enough rule breaking in the free-agency chase to write three books, but I can tell you that the time on the screen of my MacBook Air was 12:00:06 (six seconds after midnight) when the phone rang in the Back Bay condo of agent Brad Blank on Friday morning. I was in the upscale downtown Boston neighborhood with Blank, and on the other end of the phone was Washington vice president of player personnel

Vinny Cerrato. The subject was Blank's client, defensive end Chris Canty, who'd been a free agent for all of six seconds.

"Hey, Brad," Cerrato said, eschewing pleasantries, "I need to get what you're thinking of numbers-wise so I can go in and talk to [owner] Dan [Snyder] and see if it fits us."

"It's eight, Vinny, and I don't really care how it's structured," Blank said, meaning $8 million per year for a four-, five-, six- or seven-year contract. "You know the deal. I'd like to get him somewhere on a plane tomorrow. You interested?"

"Let me get back to you," Cerrato said, and just like that he was gone.

In his living room, Blank, the preppy 48-year-old former Brown roommate of John F. Kennedy Jr., alternated between ESPN and the NFL Network on the TV as free agency dawned. On a legal pad he had sketched out the teams he felt were the best shot for Canty. In order, they were: 1. Washington, 2. Tennessee, 3. San Francisco, 4. Seattle, 5. Denver, 6. Dallas, 7. Miami, 8. Green Bay, 9. New York Giants.

The ideal trip, Blank thought, would be Friday in Washington, Saturday in Tennessee and Monday in Seattle. Washington wouldn't be interested if the Skins signed defensive tackle Albert Haynesworth, the prize of the crop. And Blank

January 2001, Atlanta Airport, hustling for a plane to St. Louis, must stop for a Triple Venti White Mocha (order has to be repeated), wait five minutes, watch the flustered barista lace the top with caramel, get it handed to me with the announcement "Triple Venti Caramel Macchiato," hand it back, watch him spoon the caramel out and top it with whipped cream, ask him if he's sure this is a Triple White Mocha, hear him say, "Yes," stupidly rush for my gate without tasting it, settle in my seat, and realize I'm drinking a (pretty weak) Grande Latte with whipped cream.

This week's sign that the Green Bay Packers miss Brett Favre: The Packer Pro Shop and Atrium stores at Lambeau Field saw revenue decrease by $6.5 million, from $50.2 million to $43.7 million, from Favre's last season, 2007, to the first post-Favre season, 2008

waited. And Canty, sitting home in Charlotte, waited. And his dad, Joe, who was going to take the recruiting trips with his son, waited.

And nothing.

At the scouting combine the previous week, when it's supposed to be against NFL rules for teams to have discussions with agents for soon-to-be free agents, Blank had spoken to a number of teams about Canty, a 6' 7" defensive end in a 3–4 defense who some teams thought could play defensive tackle in the 4–3. The teams, ostensibly, were feeling out the agents, and vice versa, about what level of compensation the player might get and what other teams might be interested.

One of the interested parties was Washington. Blank thought San Francisco, Tennessee and Seattle would also want in. There were others. Teams are smart enough not to blatantly offer contracts at the combine, but some of them come close. In this case Blank made it clear to anyone asking that he expected the money to come in between $6 million and $8 million a year, hopefully closer to eight.

"Football is a game of supply and demand," Blank said. "Chris is a 3–4 end and a lot of teams are going to the 3–4, and there aren't enough good ends out there. So he should be in demand."

1:08 a.m.: Cerrato rang to ask if Canty would come in for a visit later that day. "Does he like basketball?" Cerrato said. "The Wizards are in town playing Chicago. I think Obama's going to the game."

He likes basketball, Blank said, but more to the point, Blank asked if all the rumors were true about the Redskins and Haynesworth.

"We're out," said Cerrato. "He's too expensive."

"Do our numbers make sense?" Blank asked.

Pause. One second, maybe two seconds. "I'll get [negotiator] Eric [Schaffer] with you in the morning," Cerrato said.

Not exactly a ringing endorsement. But Cerrato said the Redskins would send a plane to pick up Chris and Joe Canty at the Charlotte airport at 1 p.m., and he'd get back to Blank with details.

Blank called Canty. "How you doing, Chris?" Blank said.

"On pins and needles, Brad," Canty said.

"We're doing fine," Blank said. "I'm getting conflicting reports on Haynesworth and whether they'll sign him. But they're going to send a plane for you tomorrow. That's enough of a gesture to me that you should make the trip."

"Is there any way they could sign both Chris and Haynesworth?" Joe asked.

"No, I wouldn't think so," Blank said.

"Is $8 million going to be the best we can do?" Chris inquired.

This week's sign that the Green Bay Packers don't miss Brett Favre: Only 192 season tickets in the entire building were not renewed after a 6–10 season in 2008, the first one in 17 years with Favre not under center.

"I don't know," Blank said. "I'd press for more, but you never know."

In the next 15 minutes, Blank was in touch with Seattle, Tennessee and San Francisco. All seemed interested but not frothing at the mouth. They clearly didn't want to encourage Blank to think they'd be in the market to pay $8 million a year for a good run defender with little pass-rush impact in the 3–4.

"What's the price of admission?" 49ers director of football operations Paraag Marathe asked at 1:33 a.m.

"Eight million," Blank said.

"Be in touch," Marathe said.

At 1:42, Cerrato called back with the tail number of the Redskins plane. "N10RZ," he said.

"N10RZ," Blank repeated. "I've scheduled three other trips, but it's in your hands."

"Eric will call you tomorrow," Cerrato said. He still hadn't said one word about what he thought of Canty as a player.

Blank informed the Cantys about the flight to Washington at 1 p.m. "Hopefully Tennessee after that, then Seattle Monday, then who knows?" Blank said.

To which Chris Canty said, "I'm feeling better about this. Hey Brad, you think you can leverage one offer against the other?"

Blank said he didn't know, and he suggested Canty get some sleep. Blank went to bed around 4 a.m., feeling good about Canty's chance to get an offer on Friday afternoon.

Now, Blank has had some bad days in the business. Friday and Saturday were right up there with them. He had 10 voice-mails, five from Cerrato, when he woke up around 9:30.

"BradcallmeVinny."

"BradcallmeVinny."

And then he heard it from a voice-mailer: Haynesworth had signed with the Redskins. As Cerrato explained to Blank that morning, Schaffer told Cerrato of Haynesworth's demands at the start of the night, just after midnight, and after some back and forth (Cerrato said agent Chad Speck was talking about a contract in the neighborhood of six years and $100 million, and the guarantees and averages were unacceptable to Washington), Cerrato said the Redskins were out of it. And so he had no qualms telling Blank at 1:08 a.m. that they were out of it.

("I felt awful about it," Cerrato said on Sunday afternoon. "We were out of it with Haynesworth, then around 2:30, Chad Speck calls back, and his demands are different, and so we started talking again. I like Brad, and I felt bad about it, but things changed.")

I like how the *New York Post* never takes sides. Just sort of stays on the sidelines and observes, leaving you to draw your own conclusions about the news of the day. I remember its front-page headline about *Swept Away*, the Madonna movie that came out in 2002. It read: MADONNA STINKS.

I think the funniest post-Terrell Owens Sharpie ball-signing comment in 2002 came from Seattle defensive tackle John Randle, who said that Owens's actions were "an embarrassment for the league." This comes from a man, Randle, who once sacked a quarterback, crawled on the ground on all fours, then lifted his rear leg and pretended to urinate on the field.

Now Blank had to prop up the market for Canty. He called Tennessee G.M. Mike Reinfeldt and was astonished to hear the words, "We're not interested." So the first two teams on Blank's list had vanished. The Giants scheduled a Saturday visit with Canty, and they would be interested in him as a hybrid tackle-end, but Blank also knew they were seeing Seattle defensive tackle Rocky Bernard.

Then Seattle lost some motivation by signing Green Bay defensive tackle Colin Cole. The Giants signed Bernard.

Uh-oh.

Blank thought: My God. We may have to go back to Dallas for a year or two, at $6 million per. But the Giants said they still were interested, and Green Bay called back to schedule a Monday visit. By Sunday afternoon, with his client in New York, Blank was seeing momentum toward a contract; he didn't want Canty to get on a plane to Green Bay because his experience in the business told him that if the kid got on the plane, the Giants offer could vanish in a New York minute.

The Giants got to six years, $41 million. That's it, they said; if you don't want it, good luck on your trip to Green Bay.

Blank called Canty, who was in the Giants offices in New Jersey. "You've got to draw the line somewhere," Canty said, "and I want to draw it at $7 million a year. That's what we get, or I go to Green Bay."

And that's what they got: the extra million. All in a weekend's worth of chicken for Blank and his new, rich client, who would have liked to have been richer, but was euphoric for his windfall.

"You play with fire sometimes," Blank said on Sunday night, "and sometimes you get burned. I needed the Redskins. They pay people, and they pay people quick. It didn't work out with them, but I did what I thought I had to do to get the biggest contract I could. You can't ignore the team you think is going to pay you the most money. But isn't it amazing? The last team on my list the other night is the team he ends up with. That's what happens in this business."

Canty signed the deal (six years, $42 million, including an $8.5-million signing bonus), finished his visit Sunday afternoon and went to JFK Airport. A snowstorm delayed his departure. So there was Canty, on his first night as an incredibly wealthy man, sitting in the JFK Holiday Inn.

"I can't get the smile off my face," he said. "I'm ecstatic. It was a wild ride, but I ended up in the best place for me."

This is the kind of story that keeps me wanting to do my job till I'm 92. ●

From 4-19-99: Indianapolis will rue the day that it bypassed Ricky Williams for Edgerrin James. This is a dark day for the Colts franchise.

MMQB Classic March 31, 2003

Foul Ball

I figured all I was doing was picking up a souvenir and making a kid feel good; my readers thought otherwise

I'm a very big baseball fan, and whenever I can sneak in a game while at an NFL function I've done it. Never has this gotten me in as much trouble as it did on a sunny spring day in Phoenix in 2003.

This is going to do nothing but make you envious of me, and so I'm not sure if I should write it or not, but I relate it only to let you know how thankful I am for the charmed life I lead, and to remind you that the next time I complain about anything job-related you need to put me in my place and tell me what a fool I am.

Last Wednesday, at the conclusion of the league meetings, I had a 5:15 p.m. flight from Phoenix to Newark. Being the baseball nerd that I am, I decided to stop in at the Arizona-Oakland exhibition game in Phoenix for a few innings, in large part because Randy Johnson was hurling. And so here came Miguel Tejada to the dish. Cool moment.

Reigning NL Cy Young Award winner versus reigning AL Most Valuable Player. Here's the

In January 2008 the story of the hiring of the new Falcons' coach, Michael Smith, was broken by Michael Smith of ESPN.com.

pitch. Long drive to right . . . twisting . . . curving foul . . . deep . . . and 10 feet foul, over the fence. I thought—and I have my reasons why—what a good thing it would be to have that ball.

There was a modest crowd on this toasty Arizona afternoon. And after the inning I walked out to the bleachers down the rightfield line and looked over the fence that stood between the main ballpark and the back fields where the A's train. I asked a fan where the ball was that Tejada hit, and he pointed to the first main field, where a ball sat between home plate and the first base bag.

At the same time, a kid, maybe seven years old, asked some other fans where the ball was. And those fans pointed to four foul balls sitting in sort of no-man's land between the backstop on the first field and the fence where I was. I knew this couldn't be true, because the ball went over the fence barely foul, not 35 feet foul the way it would have had to if it was where the kid thought it was.

And so I walked to the area outside the rightfield stands where a guard and an A's official were making sure no fans got down to the lower fields and the players' parking lot. I asked if I might be able to get the Johnson-Tejada ball. The official said no problem, and I walked down, past the alerted guard, and onto the pristine field to get the ball. Behind me, all of a sudden, I heard the

A man, 28ish, enters the elevator at Westin Copley Place in Boston one October Saturday. Sees me. Stares.
Man: You like Miami tomorrow?
Me: Yeah.
Man: By how much?
Me: Uh . . . six.
Man: Should I go?
Me: Yes.
Man: I mean, to the game. Should I go to the game?
Me: It's going to be a nice day. I think you should go to the game.
Man: O.K. Thanks.

running footsteps of the kid, who'd apparently snuck behind me and got past the guard too, and he scrambled past the backstop to get the ball he was sure was the one Tejada hit.

I picked up the True Ball, and I told the kid, "I'm sure you've got the one Tejada hit," just so he'd feel good about it. And when the guard saw him walking back up the ramp toward the stadium, he tried to stop the kid, but he was too quick and slipped back into the stadium. (Just like I'm sure I would have done if I was a kid and had an MVP foul ball.) I thanked the guard sincerely, told him the ball would be put to good use, and went back to watch a couple more innings before catching my plane.

Now you know why I have the best job on earth.

Quite a few readers were offended by that story, if my mailbag was any indication. Brian Howie of New York took me to task for having "swindled some little kid into believing he had the True Ball, even though you have a job that will give you ample opportunities to get another one for yourself in the future. Karma, my friend, Karma." That was just the start. . . .

YOU'LL GET YOURS SOME DAY, KING. *From Sean Griffin of Washington, D.C.:* "Let me see if I've got this right. You, fabulously wealthy sportswriter, used your prestige and fame to push your way

"My blocking? It sucks. I'm not gonna lie."

—Cincinnati wide receiver Chad Johnson (now Ochocinco), truth-teller in the summer of 2007.

into a closed-access area so you could get a foul ball. Then you lied to a seven-year-old kid so you could keep the foul ball. Then you brag in your Web column about how you cheated this seven-year-old kid out of a foul ball, so all of your readers can share in the joy of your wonderful life. Gee, how heartwarming. It's just too bad you couldn't have published this piece closer to the holiday season—peace on earth, good will toward men, and screw you kid, I got my foul ball, so there."

Wow. The anger. The rage. I introduced myself to a guard and asked if I could get a foul ball. I walked to get the foul ball. A seven-year-old boy passed through the same gate, without permission, as the guard called after him to come back. I picked up the ball I thought was hit by Miguel Tejada. The kid picked up the ball he thought was hit by Tejada. I'm supposed to convince this kid who snuck through the gate that he doesn't have the right ball and give him mine? I had permission to get the ball I got. The seven-year-old boy stole his. And I "cheated" him out of the ball? I can see how you'd be offended that I tried to make the kid feel good by telling him he had the real ball, because I told what I believed to be a lie (though not a malicious one). Maybe that's wrong. But is it right to be somewhere you shouldn't be and, technically, to possess stolen property?

From 10-23-00: That new Larry David show on HBO, *Curb Your Enthusiasm*, might be the next *Seinfeld*.

The 2007 NFL draft started at 9:10 a.m. Pacific time. Seattle's first pick came at 5:40 p.m.—exactly eight hours and 30 minutes later. If you covered Day 1 of the draft at the Seahawks complex in suburban Kirkland, you were served three meals before the team selected Maryland cornerback Josh Wilson with the 55th pick. A wise man once said, "If you're going to be bored, you might as well eat."

IT'S STILL INCREDIBLE THAT YOU DIDN'T GIVE THE KID THE FOUL BALL. *From Carlos Sires of Coral Gables, Fla.*: "First, the disclaimer. You are one of my favorite sportswriters and I read your online and magazine columns every week. It's ironic that I write you for the first time taking you to task on a non-football item—your justification for having taken the ball and not giving it to a kid. There are a lot of questions I could ask, including why you were let into the restricted area, while the kid was not; and why you think the usher/guard had the authority to allow you to take team property. But the real question is not one of laws or regulations, but of doing the right thing. I read your initial column on this and, apparently like many of your readers, thought you did the wrong thing. The right thing would have been to give the kid the ball. You don't need it. You can get as many as you want, probably autographed to boot. The kid did nothing criminal, unless you are going to characterize as criminals the thousands of kids who through the decades have jumped fences to retrieve stolen property hit into restricted areas that only famous sportswriters can get into via the permission of a gate guard. I just wonder why, despite all the technicalities you can cite in your favor, you just did not have it in you to turn around and lob the kid the ball."

YOU ARE A CLASSLESS, CLUELESS, SELFISH LOUT. *From Chris Boyle of Los Angeles*: "Despite your keen football insight, which we actually appreciate, you have never been more clueless than you are now. Let's see if we can get through to you this time. Seven-year-old boys who sneak through gates to get a foul ball at spring training aren't possessing stolen property. They're being seven-year-old boys at spring training. Middle-aged star football writers who make a point of telling everyone that they're star football writers are egotistical and self-indulgent. When a middle-aged star football writer, one who could quite easily call Miguel Tejada himself and get a signed ball, dupes a kid and then boasts about the greatness of it all, it plays rather poorly. The icing on the cake, though, is that not only do you feel the need to defend your actions (thus legitimizing our criticisms), but you do so by characterizing the kid as a delinquent. Utterly classless. When you cannot see how pushing your weight around at spring training might be a distasteful way to beat a seven-year-old, it's time for some self-assessment."

ONE MORE. *From Greg of Dallas*: It's childish to justify your actions. You can almost be guaranteed that the classmates at this kid's school have taken the opportunity to inflict some type of juvenile abuse on him for not getting the right ball.

Here's the meal lineup that was available that day: *Breakfast*: omelet station, bacon, scrambled eggs, sausage links, grits, banana bread, fresh fruit, biscuits and gravy, oatmeal. *Lunch*: sushi bar, teriyaki salmon and chicken, brown rice, soup, hamburgers, brats, Caesar salad. *Dinner*: shrimp cocktail, carving station with turkey breast and beef loin, cornbread stuffing, carrots, broccoli, mashed potatoes, salad, vegetables, homemade cookies. Unfortunately, the latte machine was left at Qwest Field, so I had to muddle through in the caffeine department with a couple of blended coffees—caffe appassionato and French roast.

At a Starbucks on the Pennsylvania Turnpike one morning, a loud but precise woman walked up to the register and said: "Grande skim gingerbread latte, 145 degrees, half-foam, double-cupped, keep the lid off, and instead of the regular gingerbread topping you put on, please put the pumpkin spice latte topping on there." Poor register-guy had no idea what to write on the side of the cup. He went and explained to the barista, taking about 20 seconds. Maybe if it takes 33 words to order your coffee, you're getting a little too adventurous.

You had no duty to give the kid the ball, but to act as if you had some legal right based on the guard's clearly discriminatory decision to permit a public figure rather than a kid onto the field shows, at the least, a lack of judgment. Of course, you could have originally told the story without including the kid and your supposedly correct determination of which was actually Tejada's ball. That would have been the best decision."

To Carlos and Chris and Greg, and to my editor's doorman in Manhattan, and to the hundred or so others who have written similar letters whacking me upside the head until I am unconscious, I would like to say thank you for reading and thank you for taking the time to write and thank you for being passionate. I know how you feel. I suppose this will paint me as more of an ogre than before, but my opinion of the incident has not changed. And so I am going to, with all due respect to you and the others, move on.

I do regret telling the kid he got the real ball. But I don't regret going through the proper channels, asking permission to go get the ball, getting it and, a few months later, giving it to one of the kids on the softball team I coach as a reward for a job well done.

Just another reason for many of you to think: "What a pompous jerk."

Ten Things I Think I Think

The Hall Oughta Call

The Pro Football Hall of Fame mostly gets it right, but how these 10 men haven't been elected is beyond me

1. MICK TINGELHOFF, *C, Vikings.* Started every pre-, regular- and postseason game for the playoff-staple Vikings from 1962 through '78. That's taking the field for *every* one of the 259 games that count (not including exhibitions), including paving the way for four Super Bowl–bound running games. He was voted All-Pro more often than any center of all time. This should be easy. I scratch my head every year he's not enshrined. The reason, I'm told, is that he wasn't the dominant run blocker that some other road-grading centers have been. I say if a player has been judged the best at this pivotal position on the offensive line more than any player in history, and if a player starts every game for 17 straight years for a consistent contender, he's got to be in the Hall.

2. ED SABOL, *founder, NFL Films.* Sold the NFL on making mythic figures out of football players by venerating them on film. No single entity has

"We were in the locker room, so we missed that. Nobody kept us abreast of that."

—Patriots coach Bill Belichick, asked by David Letterman on Feb. 4, 2004, if he had any knowledge of the Janet Jackson "wardrobe malfunction" during halftime of Super Bowl XXXVIII.

done a better job of making the league the monster it is than NFL Films. Kids who grew up to run, coach and play for NFL teams played football in slow-motion in the backyard trying to imitate the way Sabol made movies about their heroes.

3. CRIS CARTER, *WR, Eagles/Vikings/Dolphins.* The best boundary receiver I've ever seen. (That's Randy Cross's definition of the man who caught the ball better than anyone, maybe ever, inches shy of the white stripe at the sideline or the end line.) Too many receivers with great numbers will be eligible for the Hall over the next decade, but this is one who didn't have just numbers. Carter was a great pass catcher with great hands. And I don't use the word "great" lightly in either case.

4. PAUL TAGLIABUE, *commissioner.* Let's make some sense of this. Pete Rozelle got into the Hall—which I'd never, ever, argue with—in 1985, four years *before* he left office. In Rozelle's last seven years, the game saw two strikes, shameful replacement games and flat TV contracts for three straight seasons. Tagliabue commished the NFL for 17 years with no work stoppages while every other pro league had them. He lorded over a period when 21 new stadiums were built or planned, when the NFL put every other sport in its rear-view mirror in terms of TV ratings and popularity. There is some sentiment among

Tagliabue critics that we should wait to see if his final labor deal explodes in a 2011 player strike. So what if it does? Didn't the owners have to vote to approve it? He is rightfully criticized for the league's not having a team in the Los Angeles market and for putting expansion teams in Charlotte (a relative success, though not a smash) and tepid Jacksonville. But on balance, it's absurd that he's not in the Hall.

5. JOE KLECKO, *DT/DE, Jets/Colts.* Holds the distinction of being the only defensive player in history to make the Pro Bowl at three different positions: defensive end (1981), defensive tackle ('83–84) and as a 265-pound nosetackle ('85). People who love the Jets—and some who hate them, doubtless—will never forget his 1981 season, when as a superb run- and pass-playing DE, he had 20½ sacks and, according to Jets' stat-keepers, 136 quarterback pressures. The great Lawrence Taylor's career high for sacks in a year: 20½. Even in his declining last couple of years— he had chronic knee trouble—Klecko was a force.

6. JERRY KRAMER, *G, Packers.* In 1969, 16 players were voted to the NFL's 50th anniversary team by the selection committee of the Pro Football Hall of Fame. Three offensive linemen were picked. The lone guard was Kramer, from the Packers' glory-year teams. Tell me how the selec-

I'm doing the mainly desolate drive up I-43 to Green Bay. Around Kohler, I see the flashing lights in my rearview mirror. "Good evening," an officer P. Schaefer said. "I clocked you around 81, 83 mph. You know, we've been fishing a lot of people out of ditches today because of the strong winds. I just want you to drive careful, O.K.? I'm just going to give you a warning." At the hotel, the desk clerk told me twice to have a nice night. In the morning the maid introduced herself, and did I need anything special? I wonder if all the welcome mats in the United States are manufactured in Wisconsin.

tion committee of the Pro Football Hall of Fame has excluded him for his 36 years of eligibility.

7. STEVE TASKER, *special teamer, Oilers/Bills.* Anyone who watched a lot of football in the '80s and '90s has to say that Tasker was the best special-teamer they ever saw. After his career ended, longtime special-teams coach Bruce DeHaven, Tasker's guy in Buffalo, handed me a VCR tape of 10 Tasker plays. "Watch this," he said, "and you won't have any doubt he deserves to be in the Hall of Fame. These are 10 plays that decided games. Not 10 plays that are outstanding special-teams plays. But 10 plays that you can go back, look and say, 'If he doesn't make these plays, we don't win that game.'" So I took it home, watched it, and saw Tasker leaping to block punts from nowhere, catapulting himself over goal lines to tip punts back into play, beating double- (and one triple-) coverage on punt teams to go down and blow up the return guy and force fumbles. . . . I mean, utter devastation. Now you'll ask, "Special teams? How can you support a guy who plays six or eight plays a game?" But special-teams play takes up 22% of an average NFL game. And consider electing players who don't play every snap—pass rushers, for instance, or some defensive linemen, who might play 25% or 28% of the game. If you have great impact, and

I think you won't get anywhere with me when you say that men like O.J. Simpson and Lawrence Taylor, both of whom have had post-career trouble with the law, should be removed from the Pro Football Hall of Fame. It's not the Moral Pro Football Hall of Fame. Never has been and never should be.

play 28 plays a game, you should have the same chance to get in the Hall as a great pass rusher who sacks the quarterback once a week.

8. SHANNON SHARPE, *TE, Broncos/Ravens.* I'd certainly make a case for Sharpe (and have) using regular-season evidence only. I think he's the best receiving tight end in the NFL's first 80 years. His 815 catches, 10,060 yards and 62 TDs were all league records when he retired. But his postseason record is remarkable too. His 18-game playoff career (62 receptions and 814 yards, including a record 96-yard TD catch against Oakland in 2000) is like another All-Pro season in and of itself, never mind his three Super Bowl rings.

9. BUCKO KILROY, *G-NG-scout, Eagles/Patriots.* We don't give architects enough credit in the game. Kilroy played and scouted for 64 years. Imagine a three-time All-Pro guard, three-time All-Pro noseguard and one of the creators of modern scouting not being in the Hall.

10. RICHARD DENT, *DE, Bears/Colts/Eagles/49ers.* He had 23 sacks in the 19 regular- and postseason games of 1985, when the Bears had one of the best defensive seasons in NFL history. Mike Singletary was the nerve center of the defense, Dan Hampton the fiery leader of the defensive front. But the toughest guy for offenses to deal with on that great Chicago team was Dent. ●

From 4-28-03:
I think in New England, it won't be long before Dan Klecko is as beloved as Tedy Bruschi.

MMQB Classic December 26, 2005

Family Matters

James Dungy's death provided a huge dose of perspective, changing my view of workaholic coaches

One of things I get asked (I'm sure all writers do) about my subjects is whether so-and-so is a good guy, or whether he's a phony. Absolute best, most guileless, real, considerate and honest guy I've met covering the NFL? Tony Dungy. That's what made the suicide of his son James such a hurtful thing to everyone who knows Tony.

Very bad things happen to very good people. That's all I can make of the death of James Dungy and its impact on the family of Tony and Lauren Dungy. We're all trying to make some sense of something that makes no sense.

This is what I thought of over the weekend: A couple of weeks ago, Cris Carter, my partner at HBO's *Inside the NFL*, was in the midst of a career dilemma. An assistant on the high school football team at nationally ranked St. Thomas Aquinas in Fort Lauderdale, Carter's been think-

"May be getting too big and heavy ... Very self-confident to the point where some people view him as arrogant and almost obnoxious ... Tends to hold onto the ball too long. Does not find second and third receivers as quickly as he has to."

—Prescient scouting report by *Pro Football Weekly* analyst Joel Buchsbaum, on the second pick in the 1998 draft, Washington State quarterback Ryan Leaf. Buchsbaum died in 2002. Bill Belichick was so fond of Buchsbaum that he drove down to his funeral in New Jersey.

ing about his future a lot recently. He's been offered the chance to be a high school head coach
in Florida. He loves coaching and he's trying to
decide if it's something he wants to do with the
rest of his life.

"You got Tony's number?" he asked me in the
studio one day. "I'm going to call him. See what
he thinks."

I gave him Dungy's phone number and he
called. On Thursday, after the unthinkable happened, I asked Carter what Dungy had said to
him in the phone call.

"He said 'You've got to follow your heart,' "
Carter said. "He said when he talks to prospects
at the scouting combine every year and asks them
who the most influential person in their life was,
most of them don't say their mom or their dad.
It's their high school football coach. He said it's
been one of his regrets that he wasn't a high
school coach."

How incredibly poignant those words seem
now. Imagine what Tony Dungy is thinking. Why
wasn't I there for my son more? That's what I
would be thinking if one of my children died the
way James Dungy apparently did. Suicide is the
initial finding of the cause of death of 18-year-old
James Dungy at his apartment in a Tampa suburb.

First, I have to say what I've said on so many

Non sequitur press
box announcement
in the middle
of the third quarter
during Super Bowl
XXXV: "We have
a report from both
benches that
neither team
changed cleats at
halftime."

My alltime top 10
Seinfeld episodes:

1. *The Bris.*
Half of America
didn't know
what a mohel was
before this.

2. *The Pick.*
"Oh my God!
Fred! I sent one
to Fred!"

3. *The Hamptons.*
Elaine: "It
shrinks?" Jerry:
"Like a frightened
turtle."

4. *The Marine
Biologist.*
"Save the whale,
George, for me."

5. *The Soup Nazi.*
How he suffered
for his soup.

occasions this season, and in previous seasons, about Tony Dungy. He is the most human, family-oriented person among NFL coaches I've met in 21 years covering the league. All the long conversations we've had at owners' meetings, in locker rooms, at training camps, over the phone—going back and forth this season on the merits of going for the perfect season—and now this. I can't think of a better role model in the NFL. I mean, his own players go to him for fathering advice.

I wrote about Dungy for SPORTS ILLUSTRATED this week. The genesis of the story: I was asked by one of my editors to write about something that was good in the NFL, in 2005. I thought about a few things—the enduring quality of the Patriots (overwritten), the fun-loving charm of Chad Johnson (a bit of a reach, though I believe it), Andy Reid's standing up to Terrell Owens (America's so sick of that story), the resurgent Colts (it'll be written in January) and Tony Dungy. Now that one felt just right. Early this month he was handling the perfect-season stuff with aplomb, he had conquered Mount New England, he had his team poised for history, he drove one of his younger kids to school at least once a week and he led the league in one significant category: Times Home For Dinner, Weekly, In-Season.

I tell the story in my piece about how in

Dungy's first team meeting, he goes to the front of the meeting room, looks out at the crowd of chattering players, looks out some more, waits a few seconds until finally it is perfectly quiet. "When you could hear a pin drop," I wrote, "Dungy announced softly, 'All right guys, let's get started.' The message was clear: I'm the coach and these meetings are on my terms. You'll learn best when only one person is speaking."

Colts president Bill Polian and lineman Tarik Glenn both told me they'd never heard Tony Dungy raise his voice. He is a teacher, a communicator. And it does no good to yell when you're trying to teach and communicate.

When I talked to Dungy for a Father's Day column last year, he told me a lot about his regrets that he wasn't there more for his family. The words are eerie to read now, but it's not the time to be ghoulish and repeat them. It's time to extend sympathy to him and his family for a terrible tragedy.

Having said that, we all need to understand how difficult it is to have a normal life working for an NFL team. Especially a successful NFL team. The competitiveness drives the intelligent to ignore most everything in their lives, except for the almighty football, for six months a year. It's wrong. But it's also not going to change. We always make light of a coach who sleeps on his couch rather

6. *The Junior Mint.*
Very refreshing, particularly inside a man's chest cavity.

7. *The Rye.*
Rusty eats too much Beef-A-Reeno. Jerry steals a loaf of marble rye.

8. *The Contest.*
"I'm out."

9. *The Implant.*
"They're real, and they're spectacular."

10. *The Stall.*
"No, I don't have a square to spare. I can't spare a square."

than drive home and sleep in his own bed. We either make light of it, or we talk about what a badge of honor it is and how laudable it is that a guy is willing to work that hard and leave no stone unturned in order to try to win. No more. I'll never do it again. If I hear a guy is sleeping in the office four nights a week, I'll never say to him, "Boy, you're really working hard to get this thing turned around." Instead, I'll just think: Your poor family. How do they cope when you never come home at night? Don't you feel like you're screwing them?

Last week Atlanta coach Jim Mora told Terry Bradshaw that he watched *SpongeBob SquarePants* with his kids and loved it. A real live person as coach! If the death of James Dungy does one thing, I hope it sets off an alarm in the heads of the 540 or so NFL coaches, particularly the other 31 head coaches. I hope the alarm says: "Hey, most of you have families. Go home. Don't look at that end sweep for next week's foe the 36th time; you've already seen it 35 times. Go home. Be a person." I bet that's what Tony Dungy would want you to do.

The Dungys have adopted three children, and Dungy told me that if wife Lauren had her way, "We'd adopt about six more." Sometimes bad things happen to good people. Very good people.

A first in SI.com history, I believe: On Tuesday, Oct. 20, 2008, returning to New Jersey from Boston on Amtrak Acela train number 2159, I wrote the entire 604-word top to my column on my BlackBerry. Not so bad, either. The all-thumb-job took about 45 minutes.

A Field Trip Like No Other

My visit to Afghanistan produced indelible memories of soldiers and NFL players inspiring one another

I'm a dove. A big one. Never once have I thought of making the military a career. But I've always appreciated the thankless job our service people do. When the opportunity, via the NFL and USO, came to take a seven-day trip to Afghanistan with three NFL players, I jumped at it. It turned out to be the most memorable week of my life.

I talked with commissioner Roger Goodell on Friday night about my USO trip with NFL players Luis Castillo, Tommie Harris and Mike Rucker, and I probably got a little excited about our week in the middle of the war. "Sounds like a life-changing experience for you," Goodell said.

Not exactly, but close. More like the greatest field trip of all time. Quick story: Last Wednesday, we're flying in a C-17 cargo plane from the staging airbase for the war—in Kyrgyzstan, 400 miles northeast of the Afghanistan border—and

From 11-15-99: The draft is 23 weeks away, but I guess I couldn't wait for the new century. Here are my top three:

1. Cincinnati: DE Courtney Brown, Penn State

2. Cleveland: WR Peter Warrick, Florida State

3. Washington (from New Orleans): LB LaVar Arrington, Penn State

Brown went No. 1 to the Browns, Arrington No. 2 to the Redskins, and Warrick No. 4 to the Bengals.

as we approach the border, we're over the most beautiful snowcapped mountain peaks, with an elevation of about 15,000 feet.

Air Force pilot Matt Jarrett rose from his seat in the cockpit and put on an armored vest and combat helmet. Hmmm. I waited for an explanation. As he fetched the armor plate to put under his seat, the friendly Jarrett said in a cool monotone: "Not that anything's going to happen, but what I'd like you to do when we cross into Afghanistan is to look out your window for us as we go. If you see anything unusual down there, or anything that looks like it's tracking on the plane, in as normal a voice as you can, alert us that something's up out there, O.K.?"

Not that the Taliban has any armament that can shoot down a plane this big, two miles up in the sky, but I guess it's better to be safe than sorry. My exact thought at the moment: Peter, you're not in Jersey anymore.

Hope you don't mind, but I'm going to let the real world intrude on the NFL this week. But it's the real world with a football accent on it.

I didn't sleep well in Afghanistan, on any night. I think it was part adrenaline, part decibel levels of the planes and helicopters rattling the walls of our barracks at four bases, part not sleeping as

"Me and Coach Belichick, it's more a mental bond. We really don't conversate."

—Randy Moss, on his relationship with his coach, in January 2008.

well at 50 as one does at 25, and part not wanting to miss anything—because this experience was like coming out of the womb and being so wide-eyed.

Everything you're seeing, you're seeing for the first time. Real barracks (as unglamorous and as scented as you'd imagine), real latrines (ditto), surprisingly very good food (I hear it costs the U.S. taxpayers $30 per meal), drones with lawn-mower-sounding engines piloted by pilots sitting in a control center in Nevada. We also got to feel the power of a Blackhawk helicopter while riding over Bedouin encampments 20 miles from the Pakistan border, and met some seemingly fearless Army Ranger and Special Forces troops, who have the enemy shooting at them daily.

That's what this story is about. On Thursday night, after a Q&A session we did on the base in Kandahar, in the desert of southern Afghanistan, six from our group ventured into a room shared by several members of the Army's 1st Battalion, 508th Scout Sniper Reconnaissance Platoon. Four in the platoon of 30 are highly trained Army Rangers, the others are elite soldiers. Several of them wear silver bracelets bearing the name of the late Tanner James O'Leary, a South Dakota kid and driver of their Humvee that was blown up by an IED on a mission near here last year.

I think you'd better not invite Keyshawn Johnson and Neil O'Donnell to the same anything. Remember how Johnson ripped O'Donnell in his 1997 book *Just Give Me The Damn Ball*, even though O'Donnell was the quarterback who would be giving him the damn ball that next season? Well, Johnson took another shot at O'Donnell in the *New York Post* in September 1999, calling him "a bum, a straight-up bum." I asked O'Donnell about it. Through gritted teeth, O'Donnell told me: "His day will come."

The Giants wanted quarterback Jared Lorenzen to report to their 2005 off-season program at 270 pounds. To say the guy has had a weight issue is putting it mildly. He tipped the scales near 300 pounds while playing college ball at Kentucky. When he came in that spring, Lorenzen weighed 338 pounds. Hmm, 270. Lorenzen must have wondered: In which leg?

These guys jump out of planes and hunt Taliban soldiers for a living.

One young sergeant, Jeremiah Wagner of Simi Valley, Calif., reminded me of a skinny, chiseled Rambo, with the only attitude you can have for a man who does his job, a sort of frenetic, passionate fearlessness. Their captain, Staff Sgt. James Anderson of San Diego, could pass for the late 49ers line coach, Bobb McKittrick. He's bald, 32, as tough as they come—and he doesn't have to say a word for you to know that. He just looks at you and you think, Whoever messes with this man is going to die.

This platoon gets dropped in remote regions of the country for up to a month at a time, and they set up camp in the woods or the mountains and search for the enemy. One of them talked about mowing down Taliban troops as they walked into death.

"We heard on their radio that we got 75 of 'em," one of the Rangers said. The platoon members joked about what bad shooters the Taliban soldiers were, and if they had been any good, how many more of our side would be dead or wounded.

Hmmmm. I drink lattes and write about football. The football players play football. The snipers snipe. Interesting match of jobs in this place, which is about the size of a college dorm room.

"Who's the tough guy on your team, the real leader?" one of the snipers asked Bears defensive tackle Harris.

"Olin Kreutz, our center," Harris said. "He's our real tough guy. He's the guy everybody follows. What about your team?"

They nodded toward Anderson.

"We are competitive as hell out there," said Staff Sgt. Thomas Wakefield of Beaumont, Texas. "We went out on one mission and played stickball. Just made up a ball and started hitting it around, then made teams. We did scouting reports on the guys and picked teams, and they were real lopsided. I said to the other team, 'I'll give you two dang [protein] shakes for one of your good guys.'"

"Who talks trash the most?" one of the snipers asked.

"I'm pretty good," said Carolina defensive end Rucker, smiling, sitting on the edge of one of the beds. "We're playing Minnesota early in my career, and I'm jawing at Randy Moss all game. He gets a short pass, and one of our guys just lights him up. And I just start up with Moss again. And he gets up and starts yelling, 'Who the hell are you, 93? Who the hell are you?'"

"Do the stars act different?" Anderson, the leader, said. "I mean, really different?"

"Not on our team," said Rucker. "Steve Smith,

From 1-20-03:
Ten bucks
says Tyrone
Willingham will
be at Notre
Dame a minimum
of four years.

*Willingham was
fired in November
2004, after three
seasons.*

Julius Peppers, Jake Delhomme. They're all solid guys. We draft the right kind of guy. That's the key—draft good, competitive guys, and surround them with other guys like that."

Out of the blue, the subject turned to a recent retiree. "Brett Favre is going to drive his wife absolutely nuts," said Wagner.

And that's how it went for 30 minutes, one set of teammates asking another set of teammates questions about their lives, and the other side absolutely eating it up.

I asked the men of the 508th what role the NFL, and football Sundays, played in the lives of their platoon.

"Huge," said Wagner. "Absolutely huge. This last mission we were on sucked. Just sucked. No football. Season was over. No making fun of the Cowboy fans. No baseball. Nothing to talk about. An hour felt like a day."

There's a nine-and-a-half-hour time difference between Kandahar and New York, so the Sunday afternoon NFL games kick off late Sunday night and early Monday morning here. Wagner said when the platoon was out on a football weekend, the men would call back to base on a satellite phone in the middle of the night—but mostly on Monday morning—to find out the status of games.

Asked by the *St. Louis Post-Dispatch* how difficult it was to call so many Rams games, Fox play-by-play man Matt Vasgersian replied, "We've had plenty of Lions and Chiefs and Raiders games, too, the last couple of years, so we know how to polish up a turd pretty good. Not everybody can do the Giants and the Cowboys and the Patriots every week."

"You would not believe how important the NFL is in getting us through the week," Wagner said. "On Wednesday, we start talking about the games coming up Sunday, and then we'll talk about the games for hours after we find out who won."

The discussion ended about 1:30 a.m. When Rucker and Castillo (a Chargers defensive lineman) got back to their barracks, they laid down and talked about the night.

"The way they're excited to talk to us is the way we're excited to talk to them," said Rucker. "I wish I could do what they're doing, but I can't. I'm like a fan around those guys."

"You see how intrigued they were by us?" said Castillo. "How cool is that? The way they talk about being in a gunfight and just doing their jobs without panicking . . . amazing."

"If I didn't play football, I always knew the military was an option," said Rucker. "Now I know how much I would have loved it. Ask the guys on my team—every time they do a flyover before the game, you can see how emotional I get."

"Priceless," Castillo said, minutes before drifting off to sleep. "That was a priceless night."

On Saturday night, at the big air base in the north, Bagram, we did another meet-and-greet with the men and women of the Army, Navy, Air

"I'm not Joey!!!"

—A perturbed-sounding Raiders wide receiver Jerry Porter, after being introduced on Sporting News Radio as "Pittsburgh outside linebacker Joey Porter" in September 2002. Jerry Porter promptly hung up the phone on national radio.

Our USO travel party almost got stalled on its way home in the capital city of Kyrgyzstan. In fact, without some bold action by NFL director of community relations David Krichavsky, we might still be drinking Soviet beer and trying to divine the funky Kyrgyz language. Our party of eight hustled to make its connection in Bishkek to London because the flight from Afghanistan had been late. Luis Castillo had left his wallet and computer at the airbase in Bishkek a week earlier; he figured he'd just pick them up on his return flight out. So he and USO tour manager Jeff Anthony planned to catch a later plane.

▶

Force and Marines. At all of these things, we'd set up a table in front of the room with a mike and speakers. I'd conduct a Q&A with the players, we'd take questions from the audience, we'd give away a few USO-donated prizes and then everyone would come up and take photos and get autographs from the guys. Harris, by the way, signs his autograph quicker than anyone I've ever seen. He can do it in three seconds. I counted.

This meet-and-greet was the biggest. We had maybe 300 enlisted men and women. It was sort of a somber occasion. We'd all just come from a Fallen Comrade Ceremony, one of the most touching things you'll see on any base, ever. A 24-year-old California Army kid, riding in an armored Humvee, got blown up by an improvised explosive device, and the entire base, some 8,000 men and women, lined up along the base main street at attention as their comrade's casket was driven by.

A military band played as the casket slowly was carried to a stop near the C-130 transport plane that would take the body to Dover, Del., and then on to the family home in California. The base chaplain spoke. I stood next to Mike Rucker, who got emotional several times during the week, and he was so rigid at attention during the ceremony that he appeared to be in a standing coma. Then the casket was wheeled onto the plane, and the plane taxied out; and just a few hours, maybe 12, after this young man died, he was on his way home.

Anyway, a few minutes later we found ourselves in front of this crowd of soldiers, all waiting to be entertained. As master of ceremonies, I couldn't let the moment pass without opening the evening with a question about the impact of this trip on the three players' lives.

When it was Rucker's turn, he took the mike and took a deep breath. "When I go home," he said, "part of my vision is I want to keep your story alive. I want to make sure *no one forgets about* the job you're all doing. . . . "

And then he started to choke up.

"I just . . . I love you guys," he said, and he had to stop.

"Little things we take for granted. . . . " he said, and he had to stop again, and he put his hand to his face.

The crowd gave him an ovation, long and loud. Later, the base's second-in-command, Sgt. Major Thomas Capel, told us, "Thank you so much for coming. You have no idea how much you've helped. This is a visit these men and women won't soon forget."

They're not alone.

One problem: The immigration people would not let our party split up. They were quite insistent. Krichavsky saw a situation spiraling out of control, went to the biggest cheese he could find, handed him $100 and said he wondered if there wasn't something that could be done. All of a sudden, the Red Sea parted. Yes, of course, he was told. It was determined that, for us to break up the party of eight and have six of us go on this day and two to leave the next day, a payment of $35 per traveler was necessary. Krichavsky peeled off another $280, and we were whisked through security.

Something called the National Father's Day Council named Larry King and Donald Trump two of its three Fathers of the Year in 2005. In announcing this award, the council's selection committee chairman said that King and Trump had shown "great dedication to raising their families." King has been married eight times to seven women, Trump three. Trump had three young children at home when he had an affair with Marla Maples in the '80s.

When I got back home, I spent some time telling two people—Roger Goodell and Tom Coughlin—about the trip. "You've got to go," I said. "You'll never forget it. I'm not saying it'll change your life. That's too dramatic. But I can guarantee it'll be one of the best weeks of your life, and the people you meet will be so appreciative that you took the time. That's one of the things you won't believe—the gratitude." Both men said thanks, and they'd think about it.

Three months later, Goodell went to Iraq and Afghanistan. And 15 months later, Coughlin went to Iraq with three other NFL coaches. I was on my summer vacation, in the bleachers at Wrigley Field for a Giants-Cubs game, when I got a call from league p.r. VP Greg Aiello telling me that Goodell would be calling soon, from Afghanistan. It was near midnight there, and he was just finishing the kind of long day with the troops that I'd seen seven of. I ducked into a quiet spot and we talked for five minutes. His voice sounded weary and raspy.

I don't remember, word for word, what Goodell said. What I remember was the tone of his voice, and the gratitude. He was happy that he went. More than happy. It was some combination of an I've-done-a-good-deed-and-at-the-same-time-I've-selfishly-had-one-of-the-great-weeks-of-my-life tone. I do remember one thing he said.

"I'll never forget this week."

Ten Things I Think I Think

Under the Covers

I've written more cover stories for SI than I can remember, but these are 10 that I'll never forget

I DON'T KNOW how many times I've had cover stories in the magazine. I should have kept them all, obviously. But like a dope, I didn't. And so it was fun to take a tour through the SI Vault (si.com/vault—shameless plug for the greatest sports library in the world) to conjure up memories of the stories I've done, and the players and coaches I've cajoled to sit for cover shots when necessary. These are my personal favorites.

Esiason made SI's cover six months after coming up short in his only Super Bowl appearance: a loss to the 49ers.

AUGUST 7, 1989
Boomer Esiason: "Can Boomer Bring It?"
First cover of my life. Tremendously intimidating. And the weekend I had to write the story, I left my reporter's notebook with 23 pages of interviews on a Northwest Airlines plane and lost it forever. Thank God Boomer and wife Cheryl are the nicest people on earth, and I could reconstruct many of the key conversations and stories. Whew. Imagine telling the boss who's got the cover already planned, "Uh, I did something a first-grader would do, and the notebook's gone forever."

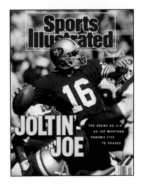

With Steve Young (8), coach George Seifert (center) and Montana, the 49ers rolled to the NFL title in 1989.

OCTOBER 2, 1989

Joe Montana: "Joltin' Joe"

I had already written my INSIDE THE NFL column for that week's issue, so managing editor Mark Mulvoy told me to go see the powerful Niners and do some research for a future story. Montana, despite taking a beating and suffering eight sacks, recovered to throw five TDs against one of the NFL's best defenses—on the road—and San Francisco got an emotional win. "You're writing," Mulvoy said on the phone after the game. Five hours later, he said, "You better have something. You've got the cover."

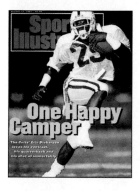

SI's 1991 cover marked the beginning of the end for the 30-year-old Dickerson, who would retire two years later.

AUGUST 12, 1991

Eric Dickerson: "One Happy Camper"

One Friday late in 1992 my wife and I sat down in a New Jersey movie theater to watch *A Few Good Men*, and midway through it Tom Cruise went to a newsstand in his D.C. neighborhood and picked up SPORTS ILLUSTRATED and started leafing through it. It was this Dickerson cover. Now that was a rush.

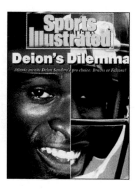

Sanders had a Pro Bowl season in '92, but it was also his most productive year in baseball (.304 batting average).

AUGUST 24, 1992

Deion Sanders: "Deion's Dilemma"

Cool cover, with half of Deion's head wearing a baseball cap and the other half in a helmet. Sanders invited me to his Pittsburgh hotel after taking an 0-fer against Pirates knuckleballer Tim Wakefield. I walked into his room and there was Sanders, glistening with sweat, swinging the bat. "I gotta get my swing right," he told me. He was frank about his role with the Braves. "They can do without me," he said. "I know it, and they know it." Sanders was always a self-promoter, but he was also an honest, sometimes self-deprecating sort.

White touched off a free-agent frenzy that was won by the Packers, whom he helped to reach two Super Bowls.

MARCH 15, 1993

Reggie White: "The Reggie Game"

Great idea. We took all the jerseys of the contenders for White, the first big free agent in NFL history, and arranged them like cutout clothes to be put on a padded Reggie. I trailed White on his free-agent jaunt and was amazed to see the teams drool all over him. Cleveland put him up in a hotel suite with two marble baths and gave his wife a $900 leather coat and a dozen yellow roses, her favorite. I remember White's agent getting off a private plane—Art Modell's—and saying to me, "Times are sure changing in the NFL."

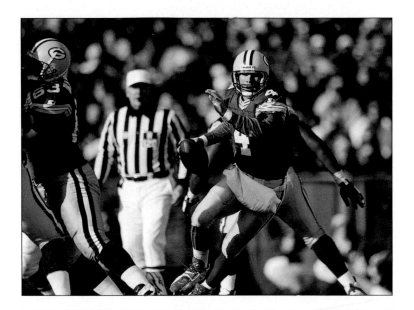

There was no SI cover jinx this time: Favre and Holmgren led the Packers to a 35–21 win in Super Bowl XXXI.

JANUARY 27, 1997

Brett Favre/Mike Holmgren: "The Missing Links"

I had to supremely coax Holmgren and Favre to go to a diner near Lambeau Field—during a game week—to take a picture together for this cover, SI's Super Bowl preview for the 1997 Packers-Patriots tilt. I'll never forget Holmgren's telling me, "Now just don't make me look stupid." And so the cover was a shot of Favre laughing and Holmgren looking goofy holding up a sausage link to the camera. I always told Holmgren: "No, you're wrong! You looked great on that cover!"

Siragusa arm-wrestled with Strahan after helping the Ravens push their way past Oakland for the AFC title.

JANUARY 29, 2001

Tony Siragusa/Michael Strahan: "D-Day"

I got two of the biggest hams in NFL history to take this photo before the Ravens-Giants Super Bowl at Ham Number One's restaurant (Siragusa's) in the Jersey burbs . . . and it only took them about 10 minutes to get the faux-menacing shot right. Siragusa would have paid to make the cover of SI.

Led by Priest Holmes (31) and Green, the Chiefs had one of the NFL's best offenses, but defense was their downfall.

NOVEMBER 17, 2003

Trent Green: "The Chiefs: Perfect (So Far)"

"You're not putting us on the cover, are you?" Green wondered when I was in town to write a story about the unbeaten Kansas City Chiefs. I never know, I said; I'm not in the cover-picking business, just the writing business. Green was worried about the whole SI jinx thing, obviously, and he didn't want to tempt fate. You know what happened three days after the cover hit the newsstands? The awful Cincinnati Bengals 24, Kansas City 19. The Chiefs went on to finish 13–3 but lost their playoff opener to the Colts, 38–31.

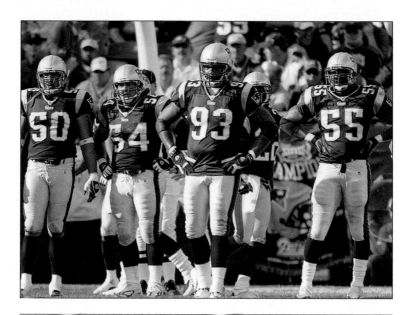

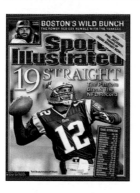

Belichick and Brady's balanced team would run its streak to 21 in a row before falling to the Steelers in 2004.

OCTOBER 18, 2004

Tom Brady: "19 Straight"

"Think how long it's been since we lost," Patriots owner Bob Kraft said, sidling up to me before the Patriots beat Miami for their NFL-record 19th straight win (and their 16th straight in the regular season). "Britney Spears has been married twice since then." I just like the cover, a classic, Montana-like pose of Brady throwing deep, and I like how the story ended, with a quote from the bookish Bill Belichick I got from him in the postgame locker room. I wrote: "'It's great to be in the history books,' said the man who has read them all."

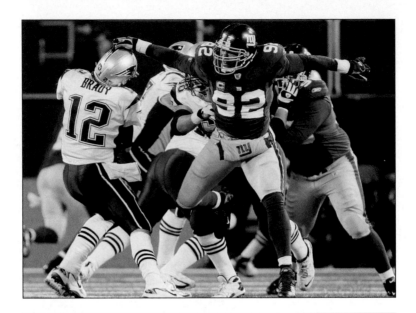

Brady's Patriots were gunning for history—the NFL's first 19–0 season; Strahan and the Giants had other ideas.

FEBRUARY 4, 2008

Michael Strahan/Tom Brady: "Can the Giants Get to Brady?"

My assignment: Pick the one factor that would decide the Giants-Patriots Super Bowl. Keeping Brady clean, I thought. To counter this, I theorized that the Giants had to let Justin Tuck loose, send multiple looks at Brady, and if they did, it would lead to "one of the great accomplishments in NFL history." Now don't let me take too deep a bow here. I picked New England to protect and win. If I really knew what I was talking about, I'd have copied SI colleague Paul Zimmerman (a.k.a. Dr. Z) and picked the G-men.

Score Another Victory for The Patriots

One of Tom Brady's most critical contributions to his team's success is not being piggish at contract time

Tom Brady's not just great. He's smart. Yes, he has won three Super Bowls and two Super Bowl MVP awards. But over the years he has also taken the Patriots at their word that they're going to build a great team around him. He knows that if he leaves some money on the table come contract time, owner Robert Kraft and his Patriots will use it to make the team around Brady better.

I also credit Brady's agent, Don Yee, for understanding what his client wants and not just blindly making sure that Brady makes the most money he possibly can. Yee knows his client, and he doesn't succumb to the gossip of other agents who counter-recruit against him by saying, "Don't pick Yee. He won't get you the best deal. Look at Brady's contract." In the end, Brady has been the perfect player for the team-first Pats, as this negotiation showed.

At the Minnesota State Fair in 2002, 36 food items were sold on a stick, such as:

1. *Deep-fried Snickers Bar on a stick.* I am serious. They fry candy bars.

2. *Walleye on a stick.* Sounds a little fishy to me.

3. *Deep-fried macaroni and cheese on a stick.* New this year.

4. *Pork chop on a stick.* I couldn't make this up.

5. *Footlong corn dog on a stick.* Ah, the old standby.

If I were the fair operators, I would have one other delicacy available: *Deep-fried Tums on a stick.*

So Tom Brady kept his word. He wasn't a pig at the trough during contract extension negotiations with the Patriots. He could have been, given that he has won three Super Bowls by age 27. We all know that Brady could have asked for anything and won the public relations battle with the team. Peyton Manning's making $14.2 million a year with the Colts, and he signed that deal a year ago, Brady could have said. You guys are high if you think I'm doing a deal for $10 million a year—especially after ESPN just raised the ante ridiculously with the new NFL broadcast contract.

But Tom Brady gets it. He knows that there have been only so many sporting Camelots in recent history, and he's smack-dab in the middle of one of them. Five days after this most recent Super Bowl triumph, Brady was vegging out in Honolulu on the deck outside his hotel room, talking on the phone about what he wanted from the contract extension destined to get done this off-season.

"To be the highest-paid, or anything like that, is not going to make me feel any better," he told me. "That's not what makes me happy. In this game, the more one player gets, the more he takes away from what others can get. Is it going to make me feel any better to make an extra mil-

I'm not saying the coffee craze in this country has gotten totally out of control, but among the flavored coffees offered at the Fort Myers (Fla.) 7-Eleven in March 2005 was Strawberry-Banana.

lion, which, after taxes, is about $500,000? That million might be more important to the team."

Read those words over again. I mean, how many guys in sports history, on the verge of signing the biggest contract they'll probably ever negotiate in their career, have said to the team: "Hey Mr. Kraft! I really don't want that much money. Just be somewhat fair, O.K.? And have a nice day. . . . "?

The mark of Brady's self-assuredness and humility about his place in the football galaxy is that when he signed his six-year, $60 million contract in the middle of last week, I'm told that he didn't even go out and celebrate. Neither he, his family nor his representative leaked the contract; I'm also told that Brady's dad found out about the deal from a reporter.

The deal is about $4 million a year less than Manning's, $3 million a year less than Michael Vick's, who's really going to have to go out and perform for that deal to pay off for Atlanta. Give or take a few BMWs, Brady's contract averages out to about what Donovan McNabb and Chad Pennington make.

Let's see how, year to year, Brady's new contract compares to Peyton Manning's deal. I contrast these deals because Brady and Manning are the best two quarterbacks in football:

"I like the Colts. We have something in common: We both defected in the middle of the night."

— Gymnast Nadia Comaneci in 2002 in *USA Today*. She defected from Romania to the U.S. in 1989, five years after the Colts defected from Baltimore to Indianapolis.

I think you would have gotten a great kick out of this exchange between a reporter and Ohio State safety Mike Doss at the 2003 scouting combine: Reporter: "Who is your agent?" Doss: "Who is my agent? That's my personal business." I heard Doss also was evasive on the following questions: a. "Have you ever chewed gum?" b. "Do you own any white socks?" c. "Do you like Westerns?" d. "Are you a football player?"

2005

MANNING: $8.43 million

BRADY: $3.417 million

2006

MANNING: $10.05 million

BRADY: $8.817 million

2007

MANNING: $7.69 million

BRADY: $10.817 million

2008

MANNING: $18.19 million

BRADY: $12.817 million

2009

MANNING: $20.69 million

BRADY: $12.817 million

2010

MANNING: $19.95 million

BRADY: $11.317 million

Let's assume each guy plays out his contract. (A bad assumption, particularly in Manning's case, because the Colts won't want to pay 18% of their cap total to one player during the last three years of Manning's deal.) But Brady's contract is so much more team-friendly, obviously. He'll take up—and I'm educated-guessing here—the following percentages of the Patriots' cap over the next six years (keep in mind that the cap will bump up significantly with the new network deal beginning next season): 4%, 8%, 11%, 12%, 11%, 9.5%.

Which means the Patriots won't ever be able to say that in Brady's prime he took up too much salary space for the team to pay Richard Seymour and Deion Branch . . . and, in the future, maybe Ben Watson and Dan Koppen and the New Running Back of 2009 and Eugene Wilson and whoever else surfaces that the team really needs.

What I really like about this too, is it says to the rest of the players that the two big leaders have sacrificed personal gain for the team. Tedy Bruschi, whether he ever plays football again or not, showed it by signing a four-year, $8.1 million contract with the Patriots in 2004 while he had a deal twice that big on the horizon if he had put his foot down or chosen the free-agency path.

Now Brady. The Pats said no over the last couple of years to big money for Ty Law and Lawyer Milloy and to lesser money for Troy Brown and Joe Andruzzi, so they're able to distinguish between what they really need and what they think, based on experience, they can do without.

To keep the turf at Lambeau Field unfrozen, 34 miles of plastic tubing lies 12 inches underneath the surface. Antifreeze is continually flushed through it.

I'm not saying that Seymour, who clearly is next in the financial line, should take 60% of his worth. But I am saying that he should look at the landscape and think about whether one more Super Bowl win might cement his Hall of Fame bust someday and make him a lifetime legend in a rabid six-state region . . . and he should consider that, like Bruschi and Brady, he shouldn't try to gouge the Patriots for every last dime.

This team has shown that it will spend to stay great by adding good middle-class contributors such as the guy they'll sign today or tomorrow: free-agent linebacker Chad Brown. He's not the assassin he used to be, of course. But Brown, who'll likely get $4 million for two years, will be the new Roman Phifer, the 30-snap-a-game guy who can play inside or outside and make sure the possible loss of Bruschi would hurt a little bit less.

The Patriots have $4 million for a Chad Brown, and they may have $1.5 million left to sign the top player cut in the June market, because Bruschi and Brady see the big picture. I know it's absurd to think of the Patriots winning yet another Super Bowl next season, but I'll tell you this: They just had one hell of a week.

A lot goes into winning. Players not being pigs is something we rarely think of, but it's a factor. ●

MMQB Classic January 21, 2002

Goodbye, Woody

Occasionally I have to deviate from football; the death of the finest dog I ever owned was one of those times

Sometimes I'm going to touch a chord I had no idea I'd touch. That happened when I wrote about the death of the most unforgettable dog I ever owned. To this day I still have people come up to me with a serious look and tell me they read the column and it impacted them. I don't know how the death of a dog can't impact you, profoundly. Four days after Woody's demise, I still had this pall over me, this feeling that I know I'll be able to move on, but just not right now. And so I moved the games of the weekend—including the infamous Pats-Raiders Tuck Rule Game—lower in the column and led with the pain of putting a best friend to sleep forever.

Time out. I know this is the biggest football weekend of what has been a very strange season, and I have plenty to say about the two games I witnessed in person (the Eagles' Donovan McNabb became an NFL man in Chicago) and the two I

From 1-10-00: I think Miami has a chance on Saturday at Jacksonville, a real chance.

Jacksonville 62, Miami 7—the biggest rout in AFC playoff history.

didn't (New England sports lore added a Snow Bowl classic) and the dumbest rule we've all ever seen (sorry, Raiders). I hope you don't mind if I put those thoughts off for a few paragraphs. I'm going to write about our family's golden retriever.

We had to put Woody to sleep last Wednesday. He was a month shy of 12. Four tumors, including one puffing out of his neck like an oval goiter, and a bad case of arthritis in his legs had left him a sick old man of a dog. I had to carry him into the house after he used the outdoor facilities for most of the last couple of weeks, and when I wasn't home because of my job, my wife, Ann, and daughters, Laura and Mary Beth, were left to do the same. I'd toss him his beloved tennis ball at Mount Hebron School up our street in Upper Montclair, N.J., and he'd catch it, feebly, and fall awkwardly to the cold ground. His legs just couldn't hold him anymore. And that is no way to live, even for this low-maintenance dog.

Everyone has great pet stories. Ours are no better, no worse, except to us. But they are ever-lasting. In 1990 Laura was 7 and Mary Beth 4, and we told them we would investigate the idea of getting a dog. Laura immediately researched everything dog. We got her a book, *The Right*

"We are the most turmoil-free team in the NFL today, and we're loving every minute of it."

—Dallas public relations director Rich Dalrymple, in an uncharacteristic lull of chaos for the Cowboys, in January 1999.

Dog for You, and she went about memorizing every trait about every dog. We'd quiz her at dinner. "Dalmatian," I'd say. "Not good around children, needs a big yard," she'd say, shaking her head. She narrowed down to a small group the list of breeds we should consider, including golden retriever, Labrador retriever and Bernese mountain dog, because they were so good with kids and so easy to live with, and not very rambunctious in comparison to other breeds. One July afternoon in 1990, we found a poor golden at a going-out-of-business sale at a pet store in nearby Cedar Grove. He had outgrown his cage, and when we took him out of it, he stumbled around like a POW who'd just spent six months in solitary. We got him for half off. Ann thought of the name Woody, and the kids loved it.

Right away he fit in perfectly. One bathroom accident before he understood. One! Affectionate but not a licker. Loved to wander, but always came home from his forays; only once did we have to send out a search party. Loyal. Ridiculously loyal. I used to wait with the kids in the morning at the bus stop, 50 yards away and around the corner, with Woody and the neighbor kids. One late afternoon, the kids weren't home yet, and Woody was missing. I couldn't find him.

Joe Namath signed a three-year, $427,000 rookie deal with the Jets in 1965. Mark Sanchez inked a five-year, $50 million rookie contract with the Jets in 2009. Namath's average compensation per year was one-70th Sanchez's average yearly pay. Oh, and part of the value of Namath's deal was jobs for his three brothers and a brother-in-law, plus a new car.

My 10 alltime favorite Red Sox:

1. Carl Yastrzemski, *OF-1B*. My idol growing up. I lived and died with his at bats.

2. David Ortiz, *DH*. I received an autographed Ortiz magazine cover for my 50th birthday. It hangs over the toilet in our guest bathroom.

3. Pedro Martinez, *P.* Nothing matched the electricity of a big Pedro start. Nothing.

4. Tony Conigliaro, *OF.* Went to the game the day after Tony C got beaned. Felt sick all day.

5. Dustin Pedroia, *2B.* You can hate this team like grim death, but you can't hate Pedroia.

▶

And some business-suited guy just off the New York bus at the same corner saw Woody lying by the bus stop with no collar on. (We weren't much for collars.) "Go home!" the man said, and Woody trotted to our front doorstep.

Woody liked me. He loved the girls. But he worshipped Ann. She was the one who usually fed him and she always had a stray piece of fish for him at dinner. She used to tell him she liked him better than most humans. "Remember when we used to play, 'Woody, come?'" she asked at dinner a couple of nights before the end. "We all stood in corners of the room with Woody in the middle and we'd say, 'Woody, come!' And he'd come to me. Then I went into the kitchen and you did it again without me, and he ran into the kitchen."

"Remember when we used to play doggie in the middle?" Mary Beth said. Two kids, a tennis ball, 30 feet apart, throwing and catching the ball, Woody pirouetting to try to steal it.

One Sunday last winter, with Woody two surgeries into his demise, we had a good snowstorm. I decided to take both our dogs, Woody and Bailey, for a five-mile walk. Much tail-wagging over that one. A mile into it, we passed a house that had its front door left open for some inexplicable reason. And a black lab, a young one, sprinted out of the house 30 yards down to the sidewalk and began doggie-playing with Bailey. "Go home!" I told the dog, but he wouldn't leave, and we were powerless to keep walking because the dog was magnetized to Bailey. I tried pulling the collarless dog by the scruff of the neck and prodding him home. No use. Bailey sensed my frustration and began barking at the dog. The dog pounced on Bailey angrily, barking rapid-fire and baring his teeth. Something triggered in Woody, a bored spectator to this point. Woody leaped up, grabbed the bizarro dog's neck with his mouth, shook it a few times menacingly and let go. "*Yelpyelpyelpyelp!*" the dog whimpered, running back to the house. "Good dog, Woody!" I said, petting his head. "Good dog!" Unimpressed, Woody looked straight ahead into the snowfall at dusk, as if to say: "Can we continue the walk now? I've got some snow to eat."

Last Monday, after I returned from Green Bay, Ann said Woody had had a tough weekend. We decided to make his appointment with his Maker for Wednesday, the day after I drove Laura back to college in Boston. Laura had a tough good-bye with Woody on Tuesday morning. And even though she loves Tufts—as do her parents—she was filled with such melancholy when I dropped her off on Tuesday afternoon. "I don't know why

6. Fred Lynn, *OF.* 1975 was about the peak of my Red-Soxness. How good was Freddy that year?

7. Carlton Fisk, *C.* Mirror image of Jason Varitek—tough, great handler of the pitching staff.

8. Jason Varitek, *C.* Mirror image of Carlton Fisk—tough, great handler of the pitching staff.

9. Jim Rice, *OF.* Struck fear into everyone he faced, and most Red Sox fans too.

10. Dave Roberts, *OF.* I don't care if it was only one stolen base. That steal spawned a title.

On the 21st night of September 2004, defensive back Earthwind Moreland, named after the R&B group Earth, Wind & Fire, was released by the Vikings (he was signed by the Patriots two days later and was on the team's roster for Super Bowl XXXIX). Which brings to mind the 1978 Earth, Wind & Fire song *September*, which begins:
Do you remember? The 21st night of September? Love was changing the minds of pretenders, while chasing the clouds away.

I'm so sad," she said. I did. Woody sickness. I had the same affliction.

Ann and I asked each other if were doing the right thing a few times on Wednesday, in between 67 phone calls I made about various NFL coaching jobs, and we wished the other would come up with some good reason to hold off another week. We decided there was no reason, other than our own selfishness. And so at 4:40 p.m., Mary Beth, who would stay home (we thought it was best, and she agreed), said goodbye. She tried to be brave. It was no use. I lifted Woody's shrinking and lumpy 84-pound frame into the back of our Explorer. He always loved going for a ride in the car.

"I'm sorry, Wood," I said, closing the trunk hatch.

"When you drove away," Mary Beth said later, "I was wishing so hard that you'd come back. I thought you'd come back."

We were ushered into one of the examining rooms at Brookside Veterinary Clinic in nearby Bloomfield. We have a terrific vet, Keith Samson, who we know prolonged Woody's life with deft surgery in June 2000. We began to say our goodbyes. But how do you say goodbye to one of the best friends, and one of the most loyal, you've ever had? How do you tell him how incredibly sorry you are for doing this? How do you tell him, with moments to spare before he dies, what he has meant to you for the past 11 years? How do you tell him you've learned so much from him about things like dignity and love and friendship? How do you tell him about the spot in your heart that no living thing will replace when he dies?

Words failed us. That's because there were no words.

Ann, voice cracking, tried it this way, cradling his head in her arms, she said softly: "Good dog. You're a good dog."

I looked him in his whitened face. "There has never been another dog like you, and there never will be," I whispered. "We will never forget you."

Now Dr. Samson was trimming the golden hair from the area around a vein in Woody's right forepaw. He swabbed the two-inch shaved area with alcohol. He'd told us death would come within 15 seconds when he injected the syringe of Sleepaway sodium pentobarbital euthanasia solution, and so we were ready when he found the vein. The injection took five seconds. The moment Dr. Samson finished, the absolute moment, Ann said, "Ohhh," and she gently let his head drop to the table. Woody's eyes fluttered shut.

Aisle seat in coach on a jumbo jet from LAX to Atlanta, redeye flight, July 2008: Three-seat row, boyfriend and girlfriend, I assume, next to me in the other two seats. They put a blanket over their heads upon takeoff. There's movement under the blanket. I'm creeped out. I try to fall asleep. Every 10 minutes or so a leg or arm jolts me slightly. After an hour or so they fall asleep. Blanket stays over their heads until we're cleared for landing. Then they sit up and get undisheveled. Don't ask me what was going on under there. I don't want to know. You don't, either.

"That's it," Dr. Samson said quietly. "He's gone."

Typing these words makes my eyes go wet. I can't help it. The powerful sadness will only go away with time. It's hard to believe how powerful it is, in fact. The death of a dog cannot equate to the death of a loved human being, can it? It shouldn't. But it does. With Woody, it does. Because Woody, those who knew him would tell you, was the best dog in the world.

There is one thing I do know. The only way not to feel such intense sadness is to never feel intense love. And that is certainly no way to live.

Well, I guess I've now broken the gridiron journalistic record for Column Most Far Afield From Football. Woody wasn't much of a football fan. He liked the orange ball in field hockey, but football . . . well, I never took him to a game. He wasn't much for TV either, so there's a good chance he wouldn't know John Madden if he smelled him. But I like football. And I'm going to take a deep breath and start writing about football now because I love to do that, and it's what I do.

An e-mail came to me from New Zealand a day after the column ran. "I can't stop crying," it said. "We just had to put our dog to sleep." I still feel a little like that when reliving that day. ●

"It's my hair, and I have nothing negative to say about it."

—ESPN draft guru Mel Kiper Jr., on his puffy coiffed 'do, in 2007.

Ten Things I Think I Think

Just Shut Up Already

If you can't say something that isn't a cliché, don't say anything at all; here are the 10 I hate the most

1. "HE'S A FUTURE HALL OF FAMER."
Imagine if all the men either retiring or verging on retirement in the last 18 months who've been described as future Hall of Famers actually were elected to the Hall: Michael Strahan, Brett Favre, Tony Gonzalez, Rodney Harrison, John Lynch, Warren Sapp, Jonathan Ogden, Junior Seau, Jason Taylor, Tom Nalen, Bryant Young, Mike Holmgren, Tony Dungy. Let's see. That's 13, and Ronde Barber, Marvin Harrison, Isaac Bruce and Derrick Brooks won't be far behind. In fact, on a Monday night game last December, Ron Jaworski called Brooks a "future Hall of Famer," and Tony Kornheiser echoed him by saying that the Bucs' defense had "a bunch of future Hall of Famers." Well, maybe he is, and maybe they do. Maybe. But the 10 Hall of Fame classes from 2000 through '09 averaged 5.4 modern candidates enshrined per season.

I think former Falcons coach Bobby Petrino pulled the most irresponsible act I've seen in coaching in all the years I've covered the NFL. One day after having been denied permission to speak to Arkansas by the man who hired him for $4.8 million a year, Petrino went ahead and talked to Arkansas anyway, and then rode out of Atlanta for Fayetteville under the cover of darkness. "I feel abused," said owner Arthur Blank. If the other SEC coaches use Petrino's carpetbagging skullduggery against him, bully for them. I hope it works.

When these men become eligible, there will be a backlog of entries already impatiently waiting, plus the classes of retirees from 2005, '06, '07 and '08. Please, please, please stop throwing this sentence around so flippantly. May I suggest the phrase "probable Hall of Famer" be subbed? "Future Hall of Famer" implies that there's no wiggle room, no doubt at all that he'll be enshrined. And I can tell you that isn't true in most cases. That brings me to. . . .

From 2-25-08: Asante Samuel could be headed for Philadelphia. I hear the All-Pro cornerback could get five years and $55 million from the Eagles, but I think once they find out no other team out there is willing to give $10 million a year to a finesse corner who doesn't like contact, the price tag could slither down a bit.

On Feb. 29, Samuel signed a six-year, $57-million deal with the Eagles.

2. "HE'S A FIRST-BALLOT HALL OF FAMER." Not to beat a dead cliché, but Nos. 1 and 2 are actually different. In 2008 I made a note of everyone I heard this about, and I lost count at about 675. The most interesting was Michael Strahan, who may well make the Hall of Fame. But it's laughable to describe anyone but a Montana- or Marino-type lock as a first-ballot guy, seeing the long waits that players have had at positions across the board. Defensive line is especially torturous. Elvin Bethea got in after waiting 15 years, Fred Dean 18, Carl Eller 20, Jack Youngblood 12, Henry Jordan 21. And Michael Strahan, whose career was a carbon copy of Chris Doleman's save for one Super Bowl ring, is going to walk in? Silly.

3. "HE'S A GREAT FOOTBALL PLAYER." The former *ESPN Sunday Night Football* guys were famous for telling us that 25 players in every game were great. Drove me up a wall. But it didn't stop there. Last fall I heard a network guy describe Minnesota tight end Visanthe Shiancoe as "a great football player." Then I threw a brick through the TV, and the madness ended.

4. "YOU'VE GOT TO BE ABLE TO RUN AND STOP THE RUN IN THIS LEAGUE TO WIN." Hey, I've got one for you! "You've got to be able to spell and type to be a sportswriter."

5. "WHAT A BRILLIANT COACHING DECISION!" Everything Bill Belichick does on the sideline is treated as if he's a white-coated Jonas Salk at the beaker, fiddling with the potion to cure polio. Please stop. I loved Herman Edwards's decision to go for two after scoring a touchdown against San Diego, down a point in Week 10 last year late in the fourth quarter. But his defense was gassed and altogether injured, and his team was a huge underdog anyway. So let's praise this noble failure but not enshrine it in Canton.

6. "WHOEVER WINS THE TURNOVER BATTLE IS GOING TO WIN THIS BALL GAME." A lie. An absolute lie. Teams with the turnover edge won 72% of games in 2008. Turnovers are important to winning, but they are not touchdowns.

This is eerie: After Tom Brady's first 11 starts in the NFL, his completion percentage was .663. After Matt Cassel's first 11 NFL starts, his completion percentage was .663. "Wow," Cassel said. "That's pretty good." Brady's record in his first 11 games as a starter: 8-3. Cassel's record: 7–4. Brady's passer rating: 91.6. Cassel's: 90.5.

7. "IT IS WHAT IT IS." I wonder if every coach and player in the league would be mouthing this if Bill Belichick hadn't won three Super Bowls in four years and taken his place on the Mount Rushmore of coaches. Belichick started this total waste of time of a sentence. I'm pretty sure it's because it's a way for Belichick to say nothing while moving his mouth. That way, he can get out of the press conference by saying less than anyone else.

8. "HE'S A DOWNHILL RUNNER." Well, he would be if he played in Aspen. But since he plays on a flat surface, he is a runner on a level playing field.

9. "THERE'S NO LOVE LOST BETWEEN THESE TWO TEAMS." The funniest time I ever heard this—and I forget who was doing the telecast—was during a Jets-Giants game. I lived in the area for 24 years, and I can assure you there was a lot more love between the teams than love lost. It's possibly the most spiteless rivalry in football, despite the proximity of the two teams and the fact that they share tabloids. Announcers think teams hate each other. Most of the time they don't.

10. "JOHN DOE'S GOT TO STEP UP OUT THERE TODAY." Either that, or Doe's got to bring his "A" game today. Or he's got to play within himself.

If Jimmy Johnson drove his boat 81 miles due south from his front yard in the Florida Keys, he would dock in Havana.

John Elway Rides Off into The Sunset

Hours after his second Super Bowl win, the Broncos quarterback was leaning toward retirement

One of my professors at Ohio University once told me, "The job of a reporter is to take your readers where they can't go." I've tried to follow that advice as I've progressed up the media ladder. So when I report, I like to try to bring you into my job with me. This isn't easy at events such as the Super Bowl, because of the crush of media. But that philosophy has guided me in the places that have produced some of my best memories of covering pro football—such as the time I wrote about here, when I hopped on a helicopter for a short ride from the Broncos' Fort Lauderdale hotel to a day-after-the-Super-Bowl press conference in Miami with Denver coach Mike Shanahan and quarterback John Elway following their second straight world title. Elway, then 38, looked out the window, mostly, pondering his future, but I got enough from

In the summer of 2007 I was asked to sign the bright yellow car of a Packers fan in the Lambeau Field parking lot. Seems the fellow, from St. Louis, parks near the walkway the players use going to and from practice, and he gets them to sign along the way. I have to say it's first time I've ever defaced a car, and certainly the first time ever when asked to do so by a Lite-drinking Green Bay fan.

147

him to know that the future probably wasn't going to include wearing cleats again.

John Elway had just disembarked from the helicopter taking him from Sunday night into Monday, to the day-after-Super-Bowl XXXIII NFL press conference. And as he walked from the chopper to the van to take him to the media room, I said to him, "Just one question: Do you know what you're going to do and just aren't saying right now?"

Elway gave me sort of a knowing grin.

"I have a pretty good idea," he said. "I just don't want to close the door right now."

Smart. John Elway the competitor is 70% intelligence, 30% emotion. He's saying, basically, that he's retiring, with an asterisk. Now I believe that Sunday was his last game ("And if it is," Mike Shanahan said, aptly, "what a wonderful way to go out"), and I believe this for three or four reasons. He didn't fight Shanahan on getting pulled from the game late Sunday night, and he hates getting pulled, regardless of the score. He took his wife, Janet, and some friends onto the field to take some commemorative last-time-as-a-player photos late Sunday night. And he sounds like the retiring type.

The one thing that worries me about the pre-

"Don't worry. It'll get done."

—NFLPA executive director Gene Upshaw, to me, on his sense of the fate of the negotiations with ownership over a new collective bargaining agreement after owners opted out of the agreement in May 2008. (Those were the last words Upshaw ever spoke to me. He was dead, of pancreatic cancer, nine weeks later.)

diction? There's nothing in Elway's life that he's dying to do. He doesn't fancy himself a pregame show TV guy, which seems the natural place for stars to slide into when they retire.

"Jim Brown retired at 29, after a great season, after being named MVP," I said.

"Jim Brown wouldn't have retired today at 29, I'll tell you that," Elway said.

"Money too good?" I asked.

He nodded.

"But you don't need money," I said. "Your grandchildren won't be able to spend all the money you've made in the last 16 years."

"Money," he agreed, "is definitely not a factor in whatever I do."

Nice knowing you, John.

Three months later, almost to the day, an emotional Elway put on a suit, affixed a ribbon to his lapel in honor of the victims of the recent shootings at Columbine High School and stepped to a podium in Denver. "I can't do it physically any more," he said, his voice dripping with emotion. "I don't look at it as a retirement, though. I'm just graduating from football." To this day, whenever I see Elway at a Super Bowl, I see the looks he gets from fans. And those looks say, "Wow! There's Springsteen."

From 6-16-03:
I think Travis Henry will lead the NFL in rushing this year.

Henry was 11th, a mere 710 yards south of Jamal Lewis.

Going to the annual scouting combine in Indianapolis every year is like Groundhog Day. Same weather (snow) and same faces too. There's Jerry Jones in his luxury bus, idling in front of the Marriott (wonder which agent he's schmoozing in there now?). There's Jim Mora, in line at Starbucks. There's Mike Lombardi, at Jillian's sports bar, watching the Friday night NBA game. There's Wade Phillips in his Cowboys pullover. A couple of years back, it was a Chargers pullover. A decade or so ago, a Bills pullover. Before that, a Broncos pullover.

▶

MMQB Classic December 25, 2006

Christmas Presence

Mike McGuire's most cherished holiday gift was simply being home with his family—and being alive

This is the column I've always wished people who think they have it bad would read. It's about the person I know who has the best perspective on life, Army Sgt. 1st Class Mike McGuire.

Christmas time. My thoughts turn to Mike McGuire, and so I phone him.

"I saw the Ravens this week," McGuire said the other day from his home in Baumholder, Germany. The man lives for his NFL. "Boy, they look good. What a defense. And then I saw my Rams beat Oakland. That was good."

From a continent away, Army Sergeant McGuire, commander of the 40th Engineer Battalion, 2nd Brigade Combat Team, 1st Armored Division, sounds fine. He is the same optimistic, level-headed, sports-loving family guy I sat with a year and a half ago, by chance, at a Cardinals game at Busch Stadium in St. Louis.

Only now, after having spent a year in Iraq leading a unit of Army soldiers detonating Improvised Explosive Devices, Mike's life is different. He has seen too much. Back home in Germany with his wife, Pam, and three of his five children, McGuire, 36, can sleep only two hours at a time, never soundly. A bomb blast that killed one of his best friends has robbed him of the hearing in his right ear. Sometimes, when he lies down at night, he has to keep a towel nearby to wipe away the blood that runs out of his dead eardrum.

And the bad dreams, about a September bombing that killed one of his best friends in the world and seriously wounded two others in his platoon, don't go away. I'm impressed that he can look at life with such hope and optimism, that he can get back into the rhythm of life with daughters Emily, Chelsea and Riley. Mini-Mike, they call her; she's eight and she clings to him like she can't let go. (Stepson Joel, 21, and son David, 19, are back in the U.S., beginning the next phase of their lives.)

"Being alive," he says. "That's my best Christmas present."

The job of McGuire's platoon was to patrol the paved and unpaved roads in the Iraqi city of Ramadi, to find and destroy IEDs, the roadside bombs planted by native insurgents opposed to the American presence in their country. It's the

Only difference between now and, say, 10 years ago? The immense media throng—maybe 15 strong in 1997, 350 in 2007. Dotcoms, scores of them, and team websites. Even college papers. I almost forgot: now there's the NFL Network, and Sirius NFL Radio. Instead of reporters staking out the hallways for players, now they're brought into a media ballroom. And instead of having a half hour alone with Bill Polian, now it's only a few minutes. Just a little snapshot of something that, like everything in the NFL over the years, is exploding.

kind of job that caffeinates you every second you're on duty, the high-wire, dangerous kind of job that makes some men so weak that they curl up and refuse to go on patrol. The kind of job that Mike McGuire will perform again . . . in 13 months.

"It's all I know," he said. "I'll start to train another platoon in January, and we'll re-deploy in January 2008. I hope the war is over then, but the reality of it is, it won't be."

The men will be much like the ones he began to form into soldiers almost two years ago. "They look just like my boys—tall, skinny. When they come in, I wouldn't have trusted them to tie their own shoes. And by the time we were on patrol on those dangerous streets, I'd trust them with my life. It comes from the bonding of war. These are my brothers. I love them like sons. I thought we'd die on a lot of days out there, and for a lot of guys, those are the awakening moments of their lives. What made them become men is the will to survive."

One of those boys turned men was Allan Bevington, a 22-year-old soldier from Beaver Falls, Pa., who worked his way up to the rank of sergeant. He and McGuire were the leaders of the group that patrolled for IEDs. "Sergeant Bevington was by far the bravest guy I ever served with," McGuire said.

I think I wonder this about referees: Why is it that, when they announce a false start penalty, most of them say, "Prior to the snap, false start. . . . " How can a false start come after the snap?

Bravery, as you'll come to understand, is a crucial trait in McGuire's job.

"We didn't have the high-tech robotics," he said. "We'd just go out on the streets. Sometimes we'd get reports from our eye-in-the-sky to go clear a certain area, they'd spotted something and we had to check it out. Was there dirt overturned recently? Was there a soda can sitting there in an area where it shouldn't be? Was there a rock or two out of place? Was there a wire visible? You see the signs, you figure maybe there's something there.

"There were a couple of ways for the IEDs to go off. Sometimes there'd be a guy with binoculars, 1,000 or 2,000 meters away. If he'd see somebody looking around for an IED, he'd activate the bomb and it'd go off. Or they had things called 'pressure switches,' and if you stepped on one of those, it'd usually activate the bomb.

"One of the amazing things about it was, let's say we'd find four IEDs one day and dismantle all of them, either by cutting the wires or by shooting at it to set it off. We'd clear the road, and the next day—eight, 12 hours later—we'd go back, and the bombs would be put back, right in the same spot. You could never relax. It was like they were saying, 'You can dismantle all the bombs you want. But we're not going away.' It is never-ending. You will never find all of the bombs.

Whenever I hear that a former coach is coming back to the profession, I recall a conversation I had with Bill Parcells in 2001 when Dick Vermeil returned to the sidelines. "Peter," Parcells said, "it's a narcotic." So is $10 million.

Because I so often rip the inconsistency of Starbucks lattes, I must share this December 2000 e-mail from Scott, in Denver: "Learn to appreciate the inconsistency of your favorite coffee drinks. Every latte is hand-made, from scratch. Each one has a distinct personality. Like a quarterback, it takes time for a barista to learn his/her position. Be at peace with your coffeenerdness. Live in harmony with the ebbs and flows of the latte."

"One day in September, a captain came to us and said, 'Hey, can you go clear this road? We know there's some activity on it.' He drew us a map on a napkin. This road was off a main road, maybe 400 meters off a highway. So our platoon goes there in two Humvees, and then we went on foot, looking for the devices. Is there dirt overturned, or some footprints?

"Sergeant Bevington actually walks over a pressure switch, and I carefully pick it up and say, 'Hey! Look what you stepped over!' A second later, there's a huge explosion. Me and my squad leader get blown about 15 feet away. My ears are ringing like mad, smoke everywhere, my gunman on top of the Humvee stars firing rounds everywhere. I look over and see one of my men, Private Ragusci, floating upside down in a canal. We yell to get him out. Private Huerta got major facial wounds all up and down one side of his face. And I look over and there's Sergeant Bevington lying there. We're like, 'Get up! Get up!' But one of the men said, 'Sorry, Mac. He's gone.'

"Now Ragusci comes walking up the hill toward the Humvee and his arm, it looks like you stuck a firecracker in a cantaloupe. But we get him and Huerta in the Humvee, we've got a doc with us, and we head for the hospital. That 15-minute ride felt like two hours. Plus, we hadn't secured the road, so who knows if we're going to get hit again."

Bevington died. Ragusci, after many surgeries and skin grafts, had his arm saved. Huerta lost an eye. Ragusci will be back for another tour. Huerta isn't allowed to do that.

"What a great man Bevington was," McGuire said. "Fearless. I still think about him all the time. They did a real nice story on him in his hometown paper back in Pittsburgh. Ragusci, he wanted to come back. It's his life. It's interesting. Some of the guys who are not coming back say to me, 'Sergeant, do you think less of me because I'm getting out?' And I say, 'No, you've done your duty. Be proud of serving your country.'

"It's fantastic being home, especially for Christmas. But it can be tough too. Pam says, 'Come to bed,' and I can't sleep. Maybe I get two hours a night. After what I saw, it can make you not sleep. I can't explain it very well, but it just is hard. And then my ear gives me some trouble. But I'm one of the lucky ones, believe me. I've got it great."

I wondered about the importance of the NFL to McGuire and his men, because in most of his e-mails to me over the last year, he has talked about how much football he saw and what he knew about the NFL. It was plenty.

"Well, we lived in the desert, literally," he said.

The first-team all-conference quarterback for the Pittsburgh-area Catholic League in 1949: John Unitas. Second-team: Dan Rooney.

Speaking from my intimate knowledge of everything pro football, I have one question after spending 75 or so nights every year for 20 years in hotels: Why do the housekeepers leave the shower drain plugged after cleaning the tub? Do they think we're a nation of bath-takers? Rise up, fellow travelers! Liberate the bathtubs of America! Keeps the tubs unplugged!

"We had nothing. And most us looked forward, once a week, to piling into a building on the base with one TV, 200 or 400 of us, and watching the NFL. The games would come on, two of them, at 10 at night. So you'd get off your shift at maybe 8 o'clock and go right over there to try to get a seat. It was my constant escape from reality, and you need it over there, believe me. Reality's not so great. Some of the guys are in fantasy leagues, and I love that, but our time on the computer was so limited that we really didn't have time to do that. So it was the games. All week, you'd count down your time to the NFL games. It was the highlight of our week.

"You'd get over to the TV, and you'd start arguing which game they'd put on. It got pretty crazy. There were so many Steelers fans. They'd go nuts for the Steelers, especially early in the season. Then they went into their unfortunate spell and the Steelers fans kind of stopped showing up, they were so depressed about it. But the highlight for me was seeing my hero, Kurt Warner, beat the 49ers in the first game of the season. I lived off that game for a long time."

Warner sent McGuire a minihelmet, inscribed: "To Mike, Thanks for all you do. God bless you, Kurt Warner." He keeps it on a shelf, right next to his bed.

"You have no idea how awesome it is to realize that Kurt Warner knows who I am," he said.

After a while, the platoon began counting down the days to go home by the NFL calendar. "Our tour was over in Week 7," McGuire said. "Just like we'd count down the weeks 'til 10 o'clock Sundays, we counted down the time to go home by figuring how many more weeks 'til Week 7 of the season. The NFL is so important to the guys over there, and lots of teams sent stuff to our guys. The Dolphins sent us hats. The Titans sent stuff to another unit."

Two Sundays ago, McGuire curled up on his couch, doing what so many of us do on Sundays: watching the NFL. Only for him, it began at 7 p.m., not 1 p.m. or 10 a.m., depending where you live in the U.S. Cleveland and Baltimore were on TV, and he sat there with eight-year-old Riley curled up on him. She didn't care much about the game, but she did care about being with him.

"Daddy," Riley said out of nowhere, "I'm glad you didn't die in the war." And she raised her head up and kissed her father.

It took McGuire a few seconds to speak after that. "Christmas," he said. "I'm just thankful I'm here."

As is everyone who has ever read about the life of Mike McGuire on SI.com. ●

MOSS MAY SEE
DOUBLE COVERAGE

—Headline in the Oct. 17, 2002 edition of *The* (Newark) *Star-Ledger*, above a story discussing the Jets' defensive plans for Vikings wide receiver Randy Moss. Reportedly, *The Star-Ledger* is plotting these exclusive headlines: SUN TO COME UP TOMORROW; STEINBRENNER DOES NOT LIKE TO LOSE; and NFL ON WAY TO HIGHER ATTENDANCE THAN INDOOR LACROSSE.

Greats of the Game

My Top 100 Players Of All Time

How do you pick the best? Start by evaluating eras—and then brace yourself for arguments

It's not easy doing a list like this, obviously. But I wrote a pro football history for SI almost 20 years ago, and used the same criteria then as now: Which players excelled in their era? You have to compare apples to apples, and so you'll be surprised that I treated some of the dominant players of the first 40 years more kindly than I did today's. It's because I think, for instance, that Otto Graham's numbers and titles stand the test of time and look better than Joe Montana's. I don't expect you to agree. I expect you to argue.

1. DON HUTSON, *WR-DB-K, Packers, 1935–45*
His record of 99 touchdown receptions, set in 1945, stood for 44 years.

2. OTTO GRAHAM, *QB, Browns, 1946–55*
He won seven league titles and seven passing titles in a legendary 10-year career.

3. JIM BROWN, *RB, Browns, 1957–65*
Averaged 100 rushing yards per game in seven seasons. Fast, furious and punishing.

4. LAWRENCE TAYLOR, *LB, Giants, 1981–93*
He made speed as important as ferocity for a game-changing defensive player.

5. DICK BUTKUS, *LB, Bears, 1965–73*
Smart, vicious and always productive: 18 sacks as a middle linebacker in '67.

6. JERRY RICE, *WR, three teams, 1985–2004*
Mr. Reliable for 20 years, with 448 receptions more than anyone else in history.

7. SAMMY BAUGH, *QB-P-DB, Redskins, 1937–52*
Incredible three-way player: In '43 he led the NFL in passing, punting and interceptions.

8. JOE MONTANA, *QB, 49ers/Chiefs, 1979–94*
Mr. Cool, Mr. Clutch, Mr. Accurate won three Super Bowl MVP awards.

9. WALTER PAYTON, *RB, Bears, 1975–87*
He missed just one game due to injury, and held the NFL rushing record for nearly two decades.

10. REGGIE WHITE, *DE, three teams, 1985–2000*
No one ever rushed the passer and stopped the run, combined, as well as the Minister of Defense.

Don Hutson was better than Jerry Rice. Hutson, a lanky Alabamian, actually was faster than Rice, whose 40-yard dash time was in the pedestrian 4.48-second range. In the early '30s Hutson ran a 9.8-second 100-yard dash. Signed by the Packers in 1935, he went on to catch 488 passes, with 99 touchdowns. My belief always has been that you have to compare apples to apples in NFL history. Hutson put up numbers that more than doubled those of anyone who played in the first 30 years of the NFL. Rice was one of the handful of best players ever, but he didn't lap the field like Hutson did.

11

Johnny Unitas is not the best quarterback ever. I can feel the crabcakes whizzing past my head on my next trip to Baltimore. Unitas was a peerless signal-caller, engineered the Colts' win in the Greatest Game Ever Played, and defined grit and smarts at the position. Dads raised their kids to be like him; men and boys got crew cuts in his honor. But Graham and Montana won more (Unitas won three titles in 18 seasons), and Baugh was more versatile and accurate. It's not so bad to be number 11. It's where Johnny U. deserves to be ranked.

11. JOHNNY UNITAS, *QB, Colts/Chargers, 1956–73*
He piloted the Colts on late tying and winning drives in the greatest game ever: the '58 title tilt.

12. DEACON JONES, *DE, three teams, 1961–74*
He actually invented the term *sack*, and he racked up 102 of 'em in a five–year span.

13. RONNIE LOTT, *CB-S, three teams, 1981–94*
No DB in last 40 years ran and hit like him. And yes, he had a fingertip cut off to keep playing.

14. BOB LILLY, *DT, Cowboys, 1961–74*
The bedrock player in the beginning of Dallas's run of greatness in the late 1960s.

15. JOE GREENE, *DT, Steelers, 1969–81*
Chuck Noll's first draft choice helped kick off a decade of Steelers dominance.

16. BRETT FAVRE, *QB, four teams, 1991–present*
Imagine playing 309 (and counting) straight games at QB. That's the record he's most proud of.

17. JACK LAMBERT, *LB, Steelers, 1974–84*
The sneer that launched four Super Bowl titles. I'm just glad he never tackled me.

18. BRONKO NAGURSKI, *RB-DL-LB, Bears, 1930–37, '43*
For years, always the best player on the field. He also threw two TD passes in the '33 title game.

19. ANTHONY MUÑOZ, *T, Bengals, 1980–92*
An even-keeled perfectionist and the most technically sound offensive lineman ever.

20. GINO MARCHETTI, *DE, Texans/Colts, 1952–66*
Unitas called this equally adept pass rusher and run stuffer the "perfect football player."

21. O.J. SIMPSON, *RB, Bills/49ers, 1969–79*
Don't get blinded by his postcareer idiocy. He rushed for 2,003 yards in 14 games one year.

22. BARRY SANDERS, *RB, Lions, 1989–98*
The shiftiest, quickest running back ever, with the best spin move in history.

23. JIM PARKER, *T-G, Colts, 1957–67*
A rare talent at drive blocking and pass-protecting; eight-year All-Pro at tackle and guard.

24. JOE SCHMIDT, *LB, Lions, 1953–65*
Once, the Lions were good, and they were keyed by the first true great middle linebacker in history.

25. PEYTON MANNING, *QB, Colts, 1998–present*
He's 34, and I'm just now starting to think he may not pass Favre on every career stat list.

26. GALE SAYERS, *RB-KR, Bears, 1965–71*
Electric, powerful back . . . and the only man ever to average 30 yards per kick return.

27. JOHN ELWAY, *QB, Broncos, 1983–98*
Always 1, 1a with Marino. Elway gets the edge, two championships to none.

28. FORREST GREGG, *T-G, Packers/Cowboys, 1956–71*
Lombardi: "Best player I ever coached." Which should be good enough for all of us.

29. RAY LEWIS, *LB, Ravens, 1996–present*
Fast. Frightening. One of pro football's alltime great leaders. Still a force at 35.

30. CHUCK BEDNARIK, *LB-C, Eagles, 1949–62*
He was the last full-time two-way player. Frank Gifford remembers him very well.

29

Ray Lewis? Ray Lewis at 29? Why not? No player of this generation has been a better leader, and his pursuit is the stuff of legend. I can still see him running from 15 yards across the field to catch the fleet Tiki Barber from behind in Super Bowl XXXV. In 2008, his 13th season, he stood up Steelers running back Rashard Mendenhall with such a vicious tackle that he broke the kid's shoulder. I'll take him, as an athlete and playmaker, over Nitschke.

37

31. DAN MARINO, *QB, Dolphins, 1983–99*
No one threw it more beautifully, ever. He was the first man to reach 400 TD passes.

32. RED GRANGE, *RB, Bears/Yankees, 1925–27, '29–'34*
He did as much for the pro game as any man. His '25 barnstorming tour made it popular.

33. ROGER STAUBACH, *QB, Cowboys, 1969–79*
Bill Belichick's boyhood idol, a Navy man, didn't take his first NFL snap till age 27.

34. DEION SANDERS, *CB, five teams, 1989–2000, '04–05*
Though he didn't tackle well, or willingly, he's the best cover cornerback in NFL history.

35. TOM BRADY, *QB, Patriots, 2000–present*
Tough call after starting for just eight years, but three rings in those first four seasons clinches it.

36. BRUCE SMITH, *DE, Bills/Redskins, 1985–2003*
He was a relentless pass-rushing force for two decades; alltime NFL sack leader with 200.

37. MARION MOTLEY, *RB, Browns/Steelers, 1946–53, '55*
The best big back in pro football history led the league in rushing in his first NFL season, 1950.

38. RAYMOND BERRY, *WR, Colts, 1955–67*
Unitas's security blanket was golden in the historic '58 title game: 12 catches, 178 yards.

39. WILLIE LANIER, *LB, Chiefs, 1967–77*
He hit like a Mack truck and, at 245 pounds, he was nimble enough to pick off 27 passes.

40. BILL WILLIS, *DL-G, Browns, 1946–53*
He helped break the color barrier, and he was dynastic Cleveland's best defensive player.

41. MEL HEIN, *C, Giants, 1931–45*
He's the only offensive lineman ever to win an
NFL Most Valuable Player award (1938).

42. RANDY MOSS, *WR, three teams, 1998–present*
Probably the best deep threat in NFL history.
Will finish around 1,100 catches and 170 TDs.

43. EMMITT SMITH, *RB, Cowboys/Cardinals, 1990–2004*
To surpass his rushing record, a back would
have to average 1,530 yards for 12 years.

44. BART STARR, *QB, Packers, 1956–71*
A pedestrian guy till Lombardi arrived, then
boom: five NFL titles in a seven–year span.

45. ROD WOODSON, *CB-S, four teams, 1987–2003*
The best blitzing corner in history was named to
the NFL's 75th anniversary team in mid-career.

46. TERRY BRADSHAW, *QB, Steelers, 1970–83*
Four rings later, I have one question: How
dumb is he now, Hollywood?

47. NIGHT TRAIN LANE, *CB, three teams, 1952–65*
The best cover man in the early days of the
professional passing game.

48. ROOSEVELT BROWN, *T, Giants, 1953–65*
He and Jim Parker were the league's best
offensive linemen in the '50s and '60s.

49. ALAN PAGE, *DT, Vikings/Bears, 1967–81*
The first defensive player ever named NFL MVP
('71), he led the vaunted Vikings defensive front.

50. JIM OTTO, *C, Raiders, 1960–74*
Amazing but true: He was the AFL's All-Pro
center in every one of the league's 10 seasons.

43

**I respect the heck
out of Emmitt
Smith, but . . . .**
The Metroplex
is apoplectic.
"Emmitt, 43rd?
What?!!!" I
understand. I view
Smith with
tremendous
admiration. What
player can touch
the ball 5,500
times, including
playoffs, and still
be ambulatory?
But I view five
backs of the last
50 years as better.
Smith was Carl
Yastrzemski—a
survivor who
played a long time
and played very
well. There's
something great to
be said for that,
but he wasn't the
force that Jim
Brown was, or
the weapon that
Walter Payton,
O.J. Simpson or
Gale Sayers were.

53

Lance Alworth was the best skill player in AFL history. A few reasons: 1. Until Alworth did it, no player averaged 100 yards receiving per game in three straight years. 2. In 1965 SI put him on its cover, calling him the game's top receiver. 3. Alworth's career yards per catch in the AFL: 19.4. Jerry Rice's in the NFL: 14.8. Alworth also helped start the AFL-NFL player war. Drafted in the first round by the Niners in 1962 and the second by Oakland, he signed with Oakland, then was traded to San Diego. Bet you'll never guess his position coach with the Chargers in 1962. Al Davis.

51. BOBBY BELL, *LB-DE, Chiefs, 1963–74*
Hank Stram asked him to do it all—rush, stop the run, cover—as a ball hawking defensive QB.

52. JOHN HANNAH, *G, Patriots, 1973–85*
What Muñoz was to tackle, Hannah was to guard . . . except a little meaner.

53. LANCE ALWORTH, *WR, Chargers/Cowboys, 1962–72*
The best receiver in AFL history. Imagine averaging 19 yards per catch, for life.

54. MERLIN OLSEN, *DT, Rams, 1962–76*
He played second fiddle to the great Deacon Jones, but made 14 straight Pro Bowls.

55. LENNY MOORE, *RB, Colts, 1956–67*
The first great receiver out of the backfield scored 111 touchdowns lining up behind Unitas.

56. JACK HAM, *LB, Steelers, 1971–82*
Mr. Turnover recovered 21 fumbles and intercepted 32 passes in the Steelers' dynasty era.

57. BRUCE MATTHEWS, *G-T-C, Oilers/Titans, 1983–2001*
No lineman ever played more games (296)—and he was All-Pro nine times.

58. LaDAINIAN TOMLINSON, *RB, two teams, 2001–present*
Set an NFL scoring record (31 touchdowns in 2006) that I doubt will ever be broken.

59. GENE UPSHAW, *G, Raiders 1967–81*
Superb drive blocker played in 10 AFC or AFL championship games in 15 years.

60. RANDY WHITE, *DT, Cowboys, 1975–88*
Imagine missing just one game in 14 years, banging weekly against 280-pounders.

61. JUNIOR SEAU, *LB, three teams, 1990–2009*
He suited up for 268 games, all played like the
Tasmanian Devil. One of history's great leaders.

62. ED REED, *S, Ravens, 2002–present*
"Best ball-hawking safety of all time," praises
one of the great safeties, Rodney Harrison.

63. SID LUCKMAN, *QB, Bears, 1939–50*
The best QBs of the NFL's first 30 years: Baugh,
Luckman. Sid won four NFL titles.

64. MEL BLOUNT, *CB, Steelers, 1970–83*
At 6' 3" and 208 pounds he was the first great
physical cover corner in league history.

65. DOUG ATKINS, *DE, three teams, 1953–69*
At 6' 8" he was the first true power forward to
terrorize quarterbacks with his pass rushing.

66. BOBBY LAYNE, *QB, four teams, 1948–62*
He defined the term *swashbuckler.* He played
hard, lived hard and was as clutch as Montana.

67. TROY AIKMAN, *QB, Cowboys, 1989–2000*
The three-time Super Bowl winner recorded 90
wins in the '90s—the most in a decade by a QB.

68. HERB ADDERLEY, *CB, Packers/Cowboys, 1961–72*
One of first big, physical corners in history
allowed Lombardi to take defensive chances.

69. BENNY FRIEDMAN, *QB, four teams, 1927–34*
He threw 20 TD passes with a nearly oblong ball
in '29; that'd be like Brady throwing 60 today.

70. MARSHALL FAULK, *RB, Colts/Rams, 1994–2005*
The NFL's Offensive Player of the Year in 1999,
2000 and '01; epitome of a versatile back.

62

**Ed Reed is better
than all the
safeties in the
NFL's first 60
years.** If you know
me, you know how
much I respect
football history.
But until Ronnie
Lott there hadn't
been a physical
safety with as
much playmaking
range as Reed.
The leading
interceptor of all
time is a safety—
Paul Krause, who
had 81. Krause
averaged 5.1 picks
per season in 16
years. Reed has
averaged 5.8
a year, in eight
years. Krause had,
and Reed has had,
two years with
nine interceptions
or more. And Reed
hits like Lott did.
He'll be higher
than 62nd on this
list in three years
if he continues
at his current pace.

74

Mel Renfro is the most underrated defensive back of all time. It took 14 years for Renfro to be enshrined in Canton, a stunning delay in acknowledging greatness, considering that Renfro is the rare bird who switched from safety to corner in mid-career, he made the Pro Bowl six times at safety and four times at corner, he intercepted 52 passes, he holds the Cowboys' kick-return average record, he returned two punts for touchdowns in the 1971 Pro Bowl, and—as a rookie in '64—led the league in kickoff and punt returns and was fourth with seven interceptions.

71. WILLIE DAVIS, *DE, Browns/Packers, 1958–69*
The best defensive lineman for the five-time NFL champs never missed a game in 12 pro seasons.

72. EMLEN TUNNELL, *DB, Giants/Packers, 1948–61*
Superb returner, interceptor and hitter picked off 79 balls in 14 seasons leading two defenses.

73. CHAMP BAILEY, *CB, Redskins/Broncos, 1999–present*
A classic cover corner with more consecutive Pro Bowl starts (eight) than any cornerback ever.

74. MEL RENFRO, *S-CB, Cowboys, 1964–77*
He played four positions—corner, free safety, kick returner, punt returner—at All-Pro levels.

75. MIKE HAYNES, *CB, Patriots/Raiders, 1976–89*
The NFL 75th anniversary team corner was a slick, smooth DB whom passers rarely tested.

76. JONATHAN OGDEN, *T, Ravens, 1996–2007*
The prototype for the strong, power-forward-type tackle who protects the QB's blind side.

77. JIM THORPE, *RB-DL-P-K, six teams, 1915–28*
The best athlete in early pro football history—and the world; won two golds at the 1912 Olympics.

78. LARRY CSONKA, *RB, Dolphins/Giants, 1968–74, '76–79*
Battering back who keyed the last perfect season in NFL history: Miami's 17–0 run in '72.

79. WILLIE BROWN, *CB, Broncos/Raiders, 1963–78*
Will anyone ever forget his slo-mo, head-bobbing, 75-yard interception in Super Bowl XI?

80. JIMMY JOHNSON, *CB, 49ers, 1961–76*
No, not *that* Jimmy Johnson—the one who was one of the league's first-ever shutdown corners.

81. MIKE DITKA, *TE, Bears/Eagles/Cowboys, 1961–72*
He's a stogie-chomping caricature now, but no better blocking TE ever roamed the gridiron.

82. PAUL WARFIELD, *WR, Browns/Dolphins, 1965–77*
A classic deep threat and possession receiver, he scored 85 touchdowns for defense-first teams.

83. FRAN TARKENTON, *QB, Vikings/Giants, 1961–78*
When he retired he had thrown for more yards (47,003) than any quarterback in NFL history.

84. TED HENDRICKS, *LB, three teams, 1969–83*
A great edge pass rusher and the best kick blocker of alltime: 25 blocked kicks, 26 interceptions.

85. LEO NOMELLINI, *DT-T, 49ers, 1950–63*
Early run stuffer–pass rusher extraordinaire who played in every Niners game for 14 years.

86. KELLEN WINSLOW, *TE, Chargers, 1979–87*
Prototype for today's athletic receiver TE; 1981 playoff game at Miami is the stuff of legend.

87. RAY NITSCHKE, *LB, Packers, 1958–72*
He made but one Pro Bowl but was named to both the NFL's 50th and 75th anniversary teams.

88. CRIS CARTER, *WR, three teams, 1987–2002*
Best boundary receiver post-Berry, best hands of his era; only Jerry Rice caught more passes.

89. LARRY WILSON, *S, Cardinals, 1960–72*
Revolutionized the position by being its first regular blitzer—and he picked off 52 passes.

90. STEVE YOUNG, *QB, Bucs/49ers, 1985–99*
Great running QB won six passing titles and threw a record six TD passes in Super Bowl XXIX.

Mike Ditka should be celebrated most as a blocker—not as a Super Bowl–winning coach or as a human billboard. I had the pleasure one day at NFL Films a few years ago of seeing six or eight Ditka blocks. Devastating. No one I've seen other than Mark Bavaro combined the ability to lay out a linebacker or safety with having good hands at the tight end position. It saddens me to see how people hoist beers to Ditka for being a fiery coach or spokesman for just about everything— instead of for what he did best in the world.

100

That's right, Doug Flutie. My rule with this list is you have to play some in the NFL. Which Flutie did, for parts of 14 years in Chicago, New England, Buffalo and San Diego. He played well enough to earn Comeback Player of the Year honors with Buffalo—and to have a cereal (Flutie Flakes) named after him—in 1998. But he's here because north of the border he was the most electric player ever, earning six MVP awards (called the Most Outstanding Player Award) in his eight-year career in Canada, where he ran for 66 touchdowns and averaged 34 TD passes a year.

91. MIKE SINGLETARY, *LB, Bears, 1981–92*
The nerve center of Buddy Ryan's 46 Defense and one of the most intense players ever.

92. MIKE WEBSTER, *C, Steelers/Chiefs, 1974–90*
An undersized block of granite who led four Steelers Super Bowl offenses on and off field.

93. ARNIE HERBER, *QB, Packers/Giants, 1930–40, '44–45*
He won three passing titles in aerial game's first decade, the '30s, then led Giants to '44 title game.

94. RICHARD DENT, *DE, four teams, 1983–97*
MVP of Super Bowl XX terrorized quarterbacks with 23 regular- and postseason sacks in 1985.

95. JOE NAMATH, *QB, Jets/Rams, 1965–77*
Unitas had the biggest win ever by a QB. Namath had the second—and helped force the merger.

96. TONY DORSETT, *RB, Cowboys/Broncos, 1977–88*
Edges the other RBs (Dickerson, Allen, Martin, Bettis) because he would make defenders miss.

97. MORTEN ANDERSEN, *K, five teams, 1982–2004, '06–07*
It pains me to not pick Vinatieri, but touchbacks and edge in 50-yard FGs (40 to 10) win the spot.

98. STEVE LARGENT, *WR, Seahawks, 1976–89*
The first man to catch 800 passes and 100 touchdowns—and he did it on a bad ball club.

99. STEVE TASKER, *WR, Oilers/Bills, 1985–97*
No special-teamer approaches his impact on the game; a seven-time Pro Bowl kamikaze pilot.

100. DOUG FLUTIE, *QB, nine teams, 1985–2005*
Gotta have fun with this: In three pro leagues he threw for 6,704 more yards than John Elway.

December 11, 2000

Out on the Range with Brett Favre

While the future Hall of Famer hit golf balls, he talked about hunting, television and underwear sabotage

So I've written a little about Brett Favre. Which, of course, I've gotten a lot of guff for. I'm in bed with Favre ... I've gotten too close to him to see his flaws ... you get the idea.

Here's how it all got started: In 1995 I got Mike Holmgren, then the Green Bay coach, to agree to let me to write a no-holds-barred story on a week inside the Packers. I'd join them Monday morning, have the run of the offices during the week and the locker room at all times, and I'd make my own arrangements to spend private time with players at their homes at night. When I arrived in Green Bay I met Favre, the young quarterback on the verge of something good—it seemed—and the first thing he said to me was, "What? Nothing to write about Bledsoe this week?" He said it with a smile, but as a pointed reference that we in the East like our East-

They just barely missed the cut on my list of the greatest alltime players:

101. Eric Dickerson, RB, *four teams, 1983–93*

102. Yale Lary, S-P, *Lions, 1952–64*

103. Dwight Stephenson, C, *Dolphins, 1980–87*

104. Earl Campbell, RB, *Oilers/Saints, 1978–85*

105. Art Shell, T, *Raiders, 1968–82*

106. Steve Hutchinson, G, *Seahawks/Vikings 2001–present*

107. Dan Fouts, QB, *Chargers, 1973–87*

108. Adam Vinatieri, K, *Patriots/Colts, 1996–present*

109. Paul Krause, S, *Redskins/Vikings, 1964–79*

110. Jim Kelly, QB, *Bills, 1986–96*

I think the final 10 players on my Alltime Top 100 made for the toughest calls. Simple reason: There are 100 more who could be on this list. Steve Van Buren, George Blanda, Henry Jordan, Walter Jones, Michael Irvin, Bob Brown, Charley Taylor, Jerome Bettis, Dante Lavelli. . . . At the end of the day I had to pick the men who I felt had the biggest impact for the longest period. Projects like this are always fun because you're never right. No one's right. So let's argue.

ern players, and Drew Bledsoe was the hot young quarterback at the time. I told him what I was in town to do, and he said, Fine, you've got me as much as you want, and feel free to come by the house.

So I did—three times that week, for three or four hours at a clip. He and fiancée Deanna Tynes and eight-year-old daughter Brittany had a happy life, from the looks of it. The next spring, of course, I kicked myself for not noticing any signs of his addiction to Vicodin. "Nobody knew but Deanna," he told me the next year. "I was pretty good at hiding it."

So that week started a welcome-mat of a relationship that I had with the Favre family. One day late in 2000 I met him before a game in Green Bay and, for 50 or 60 minutes, I asked, and he spewed.

Packers players' lounge, 1:30 p.m. Saturday. Brett Favre fetching a Gatorade from the cooler. "Fifteen questions," I say. "Fifteen minutes."

"Fine," he says. "I can hit some golf balls while we talk."

And so we head over to the Don Hutson Center across the street from the stadium. Favre drops 70 balls on the AstroTurf, pulls out his 60-degree lob wedge and doesn't wait for the first question. "Love this," he says. "I'm so into golf. Not being able to play this time of year drives me crazy. So I come in here and hit balls."

1. Why golf?

Favre: Because no one's conquered it, ever. The same club you hit perfect one day you'll shank 'em with the next. Every club's a challenge. Every shot's a challenge. That's why Tiger Woods is so great. He hits so many different shots so masterfully. He's like Deion Sanders and Randy Moss—he's ahead of his time, and everyone's gonna have to work to catch up.

2. What's your best day in golf?

Favre: Last Easter weekend in Biloxi, Miss. Shot a 66. Broadwater Golf Club, playing with a bunch of guys. Now, I'm not that good. I'm the type of guy who can shoot a 71 one day, an 80 the next. But that day was perfect.

3. You play a lot, right?

Favre: I joined Oneida [Golf & Country Club] last year and I was there so much that I got to be like Norm from *Cheers*. You know, he walks in the place and everybody says, "Norm!" That's how much I'm at Oneida. And I'll put on *The Golf Channel* at 2 o'clock in the morning and maybe pick up a tip on how to hit a wedge.

4. And now you're into hunting?

Favre: I love hunting. Tell you a story. Before the Monday night game against the Vikings a few weeks ago, we practiced Sunday morning. Beautiful day. About 60, sunny. Oneida was jammed. It

"It is a pleasure to be in the presence of so many Giants fans, all of whom I believe are unarmed."

—NBC News anchor Brian Williams, a native New Jerseyan and Giants fan, at a March of Dimes luncheon in December 2008, days after receiver Plaxico Burress accidentally shot himself at a Manhattan nightclub.

played so slow I only made nine holes. We had to be at the hotel for meetings at 7 o'clock, so I decided to hunt for a couple of hours. I've got a tree stand about 45 minutes from here. I got in it about 3:45. I had a bow with me. Within 10 minutes, a beautiful eight-point buck came right underneath me. I hit it right in the back. It ran off, and I waited a minute, then I found it, up against a tree. I dragged it out of the woods and put it in the truck. Blood all over the back of the truck. And I got to the hotel right on time. I'm a mess. People wonder what's happened to me. I'm like: "It's been a great day. Touchdown passes at practice this morning, golf in the afternoon, and an eight-point buck a couple hours ago. How was your day?"

5. Have golf and hunting taken the place of your old vices?

Favre: Even if I wanted to party—and I don't—when would I squeeze it in?

6. Who should be President?

Favre: That's one question I ain't got a clue about. Democrat, Republican, who gives a crap? We should all be thankful to live in America.

7. What's your favorite TV show?

Favre: I don't remember the last time I watched prime-time TV. I watch *The Learning Channel*, the *Discovery Channel*, *Animal Planet* and on Friday, Saturday and Sunday I watch *National Geographic*

Tampa Bay had a 325-pound tackle named Sam Lightbody on its 2006 training camp roster.

on CNBC. I like Boyd Matson. Now, you asked me about the damn Presidential crap in Florida, that's been preempting my *National Geographic* show. That pisses me off. The other day, I saw a real good show called *The Kingdom of the Snake.* Deanna said, "I'm not watching a show on snakes." I said, "Well, I'll go in the other room, then."

8. Why are you so good when it's cold? (The Packers, with Favre quarterbacking on Sunday, ran their record to 26–0 when it's 34° or colder.)

Favre: Hey, I get cold too. I freeze my rear end off. But I always think, "If it's going to be cold, the receivers' hands are gonna be cold. Maybe I'll take a little something off the ball, make it a little more catchable." I concentrate more. But I think it's also because I don't let it bug me. The other night, we've got two or three inches of snow on the driveway. I go out to shovel in shorts and clogs. I'm out there for two hours. I guess I could pay somebody to do that, couldn't I? Deanna at one point calls out to me, "You probably ought to put some pants on." Probably. I'm too lazy. If you're gonna get adjusted to this weather, you've got to brave it.

9. What's your best prank of the year?

Favre: Had to be when I pulled down [special-teams coach] Frank Novak's pants after practice one day. Classic. Every day somebody breaks us down after practice—finishes by saying some-

A few days after Boston won the 2004 World Series, I wore a Red Sox–logoed fleece to breakfast at the Seattle Westin. Guy in the elevator had a Red Sox cap and smiled broadly at me. Waitress in the coffee shop said: "I couldn't get enough of that Yankees series!" Walking out of the hotel, I encountered three Japanese men looking at a map. One smiled at me. "*Schee-ling,*" he said, nodding quickly. I said, "Yes." I was three time zones away from Franconaville. Felt like three miles.

thing. So this day I say, 'Frank, break us down!' He loves that. He gets so fired up. So we're getting ready to say, "One-two-three, *Team!*" and I pull Frank's pants down, right to his ankles. He's butt naked. He's just shocked. Everybody's whacking him on the rear end, and he's staring at me. Can't believe it.

10. Last movie you saw?

Favre: *Men of Honor*. Robert De Niro and Cuba Gooding Jr. Great movie. They both deserve a damn Oscar.

11. How's it having a baby daughter, Breleigh?

Favre: She's 17 months now. She's the greatest. Walked at 11 months. Talking now. And anything with Packers stuff on it, that's Da-Da. She saw Vonnie Holliday on TV and says, "Da-Da." We drove by Lambeau Field the other day and she saw the stadium and said, "Da-Da."

12. What's on the CD player in your car?

Favre: Tim McGraw. *All I Want*, I think. We're friends. We've got a lot in common. Both from down South, both have to pinch ourselves to believe how lucky we are.

13. Can you explain why there is green writing on your underwear?

Favre: Damn Hasselbeck and Wuerffel. [Matt, the backup QB and Danny, number 3.] I come in one day and they've autographed my underwear.

One cheek's got "With love, Matt Hasselbeck." The other's got, "All the best, Danny Wuerffel." Still I wear 'em all the time. One of my best pair. One of my only pairs. Bottom line is, the more money I get, the worse I dress. Money's not too big a thing with me. I don't even have an ATM card.

14. Greatest pass of your life?

Favre: Has to be the 1994 playoff at Detroit, rolling left and throwing that bomb to Sterling Sharpe [with 55 seconds left in what became a 28–24 win]. He lined up on the wrong side, you know. After the game, Mike [Holmgren] said, "I don't know how you found him. I'm just glad you did."

15. You want to finish your career here?

Favre: Definitely. If in two years, say, they want to trade me, I'd probably walk away. Retire.

FIVE BONUS QUESTIONS

Bonus 1. Who gets your Heisman vote?

Favre: Probably [Florida State's Chris] Weinke. Age means nothing. That TCU back [LaDainian Tomlinson] would be second. He's amazing.

Bonus 2. Who's the NFL MVP?

Favre: Carnell Lake.

Inside joke. In 1997, when Favre tied Barry Sanders for his third MVP, I cast a controversial vote for Lake, who'd shuttled between corner

As I exited a United Airlines flight from Newark to Chicago at O'Hare, a fellow in the row behind me said, "You work for ESPN, don't you?" I said, "No, I work for SPORTS ILLUSTRATED." He said, "You look just like the ESPN guy. Anyone ever tell you that?" I didn't know what to say, so I just shrugged.

My alltime
Top 10 concerts

1. Bruce
Springsteen,
Athens, Ohio,
April 1976

2. U2,
East Rutherford, N.J.,
June 2001

3. Springsteen,
Lexington, Ky.,
Nov. 1984

4. Springsteen,
Albany, N.Y.,
Nov. 2007

5. Elton John,
Foxborough, Mass.,
July 1976

6. Steely Dan,
Irvine, Calif.,
Sept. 1993

7. Tracy Chapman,
Holmdel, N.J.,
July 1997

8. Springsteen,
Denver, Sept. 2002

9. Elvis Costello,
Bethlehem, Pa.,
April 1987

10. U2
New York City,
Oct. 2005

and safety and played both positions at an all-pro level for Pittsburgh. Favre, though he's truly not mad about it, will never let me forget it.

Bonus 3. You still love it?

Favre: I do. This is a fun year. People say, "Don't you get frustrated, not being as good a team as you were?" Hey, I've been at the top, and I can still play with anybody. Teams can't stay at the top in the NFL today. We'll be back. And in order to enjoy the highs, you've got to experience the lows. It might be easy to get down at times, being 6–7. But I won't get frustrated. They pay me to handle things. If I don't handle things, all hell breaks loose.

Bonus 4. And when you retire?

Favre: I'll be down in Hattiesburg. You'll never find me. You know the HBO *Where Are They Now?* segments on *Inside the NFL*? They'll do one on me, but they'll have to get Robert Stack, like on *Unsolved Mysteries*. I'll disappear.

Bonus 5. You've thrown 251 touchdown passes. Marino's retired with 420. You're 31. Will you play long enough to catch him?

Favre: Who cares? Doesn't matter.

Fifteen minutes became two hours. That's how it usually is with Favre.

And that's why he's my favorite interview from 25 years on the beat. ●

May 5, 2003

Prep Squad

One classic softball game showed me all I ever needed to know about the value of high school sports

My wife and I moved to Boston last year. It's the first time in my 52-year life that I've lived somewhere other than the suburbs. We decided to move not because we fell out of love with Montclair, N.J.— we haven't at all, and we'll always love Montclair as our adopted hometown.

Just before we moved, I walked through the backyard one last time. I looked down in mid-yard and saw a deeply imbedded white pitching rubber and thought: Maybe I should take it out. But I didn't. I couldn't bring myself to remove it, and I hope it never comes out.

That's the pitching rubber Mary Beth King used to practice the craft of her youth, with me catching and calling balls and strikes, going back to fourth grade. We had this deal that she could go inside if she threw five straight strikes—which, until sixth or seventh grade, was the impossible dream. But she worked at it, through a broken growth plate in her pitching elbow and severe rotator cuff tendinitis. (I admit it—I pulled a string or two to get Dr. James

"I'm looking forward to getting to know the beat writers here. You're probably different than the people that write for the *Enquirer* or some of the other papers up in New York."

—Tight end Jeremy Shockey, meeting the press for the first time in New Orleans, in July 2008.

Going into Draft Day 2009, the Patriots held four picks in the first two rounds (No. 23, 34, 47 and 58). The players picked in those four spots in the 2008 draft signed various multiyear contracts that paid them a combined total of $4.9 million a year, of which $14.11 million was guaranteed. By comparison, the eighth pick of the 2008 draft, defensive end Derrick Harvey, signed a five-year contract with the Jaguars that paid him an average of $4.6 million a year, of which $17.47 million was guaranteed. In essence, the way the NFL pays rookies, the eighth pick is equivalent to the 23rd, 34th, 47th and 58th. Insane.

Andrews to look at the MRI of the fracture in her elbow. And he agreed with my Jersey orthopedist. It would heal just fine with eight weeks of rest.) But seeing that pitching rubber made me as emotional as anything about leaving our home of 18 years.

One other memory: I took Mary Beth's team in seventh grade to a tournament in Richmond, and along the way we stopped to play a game in Ashburn, Va., a couple of miles from Redskin Park. Charlie Casserly, then Washington's G.M., stopped by to watch the game. Mary Beth was wild that night, walking six or seven in three innings before I pulled her. "She'll be all right," Casserly said. "She's got the one thing you can't teach—speed. She throws really hard. She can work on her control." He turned out to be prophetic. Four springs later she was at the epicenter of one of the best games in any sport that I've ever seen.

On Saturday night, about 9 o'clock, Montclair High School softball historian/superfan Jim Zarrilli asked me, "Well, Pete, you've been to a lot of sporting events in your life. Does this one rank in the top five?"

"Jim," I said, "this might be in the top one."

Oh no. He's doing it again. He's writing about his daughter's softball team! At the top of the column! Why is he putting us through this again? He just can't help himself when it comes to writing about this personal stuff, can he?

No. He can't.

This is my week to chronicle a compelling event in a lot of lives, the big Essex County Softball Tournament quarterfinal match between third-seeded Montclair (12–4), with your favorite southpaw, junior pitcher Mary Beth King, and sixth-seeded Cedar Grove (13–4). This is a rematch of the game I wrote about last year in my column, when Mary Beth and her good friend and longtime off-season–pitching-lesson partner Kaitlyn Sweeney of Cedar Grove dueled and Montclair came out with a 2–0 win. Kaitlyn's a great kid. I coached her on a summer team when she was in seventh grade, and our families are friends. I was proud to write her a letter of college recommendation, and she'll be going to Penn State in the fall.

Now for the rematch. County tournaments in New Jersey are special, and the one in our county, a few miles west of the Meadowlands, seems particularly intense. Many of the girls grow up playing softball against the same towns in travel leagues and higher-profile summer ball. Last Monday, for instance, Montclair beat Belleville 2–1, and Mary Beth pitched. She's been playing against Belleville since fifth grade and pitching

Cleveland guard Pork Chop Womack's given name is Floyd, but no one calls him that. He was nicknamed Pork Chop not long after birth because his mom thought he resembled a local wrestler in Cleveland, Miss., Pork Chop Cash. Imagine getting ready for school on a hectic morning in the Womack home when Pork Chop was just a little Porker. Little Pork Chop is late, and Mom yells up the stairs: "Pork Chop! *Pork Chop!* Hurry up or your bacon will get cold!"

In the summer of 2007, I drove across half of America, from Montclair to Mankato, Minn., in 11 days, 1,831 miles in the car. (O.K., there was one prop plane job from Cleveland to Lexington somewhere in there.) I still remember the sky across northern Wisconsin at dusk, the sumptuous walleye sandwich in River Falls, Wis., the tiny field in Batavia, N.Y., hosting a New York–Penn League game between Jamestown and Batavia. Never, ever wonder what my favorite time of the year in the football-coverage business is. It's the three weeks of summer when training camp kicks off.

against Belleville since sixth grade, and she'd never been on a winning side against any of the Belleville teams. This wasn't a county tournament game, but after years of playing the same kids, all these games against local foes become a big deal.

Anyway, these games draw 200 or 300 people minimum, and my guess is that Saturday afternoon's contest at Montclair's field drew about 400. These county neighbors are two excruciatingly evenly matched teams. Both play low-scoring games, boast good infield defense and try to make their limited hits count. I was expecting a 2–1 game, or even 1–0. On the mound for Cedar Grove was its alltime winningest pitcher, Sweeney, who is tall and angular, technically perfect and first-team all-county. It also had the returning all-state shortstop, Holly Calcagno, who is the best hitter Mary Beth has ever faced. Calcagno is headed to UConn on athletic scholarship. We have the all-county catcher, Jess Sarfati, who's headed to play at Bates, and a Jeteresque shortstop, Kaitlin Giannetti, who is headed to play soccer at Johns Hopkins. And Mary Beth, who entered the game 6–2 with a 0.79 ERA. She's a gritty kid. The rest of the team plays pretty soundly behind her and she doesn't let the dam burst.

Cedar Grove in black and gold, on the first-base bench behind the clamshell backstop. Montclair in white tops and blue shorts. The noise started from both benches at 4 p.m., and I don't remember it stopping until it was near sundown.

Calcagno led off, and Mary Beth went fastball-change to start her 0–2. But on a 2–2 pitch, Calcagno hit a bomb 15 feet over our leftfielder's head. Julie Vreeland went back and almost got it, but it ticked off her webbing. Triple. "I threw a riser that just didn't rise," Mary Beth reported later. Calcagno hopped on the third-base bag four times, clapping her hands hard. Our infield played in to cut the run off (one run is everything in this game), and their second hitter blooped a humpback infield pop that landed almost on second base. Euphoria for the Panthers. The game was three minutes old and they had the golden run. Mary Beth finished the inning strikeout-strikeout-popout, but after a half-inning, Mary Beth thought, "We might be in trouble." Giannetti took care of that. Leading off the Montclair first, she lined a screamer up the left-centerfield gap. It got by their leftfielder, and she sprinted around the bases. Homer. Wow. Two leadoff batters. Two runs.

Amazing how symmetrical this game became. No runner reached third over the next five innings. Sweeney has an outside sinker that baffles

My buddy John Gault has a great theory on the decline of Starbucks as a business giant, and it has a lot to do with cannibalization. He works at the old NASDAQ building down on Wall Street. "When I'm outside my building," he said, "I can get to three Starbucks in 20 seconds. Starbucks is like so many big companies in the last 15 years. It's growth, growth, growth. It makes no sense to have all these stores within walking distance of each other. Would you put three gas stations next to each other? Three McDonald's next to each other? It's crazy."

In 2006, the Saints drafted USC running back Reggie Bush second overall to put a spark into their return, running and passing games. In total bonuses, the Saints paid Bush $25,325,000 in guaranteed money. In 2007, the Saints signed Illinois running back Pierre Thomas, undrafted after 255 players were chosen, as a free agent. The Saints paid Thomas a $5,000 signing bonus. Bush averaged 3.8 yards per carry in 2008; Thomas averaged 4.8.

righty hitters, including Mary Beth, who entered the game 18 for 39 at the plate but went strikeout-single-strikeout in her first three times up. "Kaitlyn is incredible," Mary Beth said at dinner that night. "She's the best pitcher I face."

In the seventh, doom for the home team. With one out, a Cedar Grove batter reached on an infield error. The Panthers followed with a cue shot over the second baseman's head and an infield single. Cedar Grove, 2–1. Fifteen kids on their sideline broke the high-jump record when the go-ahead run crossed home plate. Now, with two out and a runner on second, Calcagno came up. Walk her, I'm thinking. *Walk her!* Our coach, Tricia Palmieri, has instilled something in our kids about the other team never, ever, ever being better. "I don't care who it is," she said later. "We're going right after her." Calcagno was triple-popout-single to that point. Mary Beth had her 2–2. *Ping!* Sharp one-hopper to Giannetti, throw to first, inning over.

Bottom of the seventh. Game and county pride on the line. Walk, sacrifice. One out. Margot Vreeland, our senior rightfielder and resident pepperpot, then lined a sinking shot to center. Their centerfielder went for the shoestring catch (our runner was holding), and the ball managed to get past her. Euphoriaville!

Softball's a seven-inning game, so now it's extra innings. In this sport it's not unusual for pitchers to throw into extra innings. And in this game, no reliever ever warmed up. I don't buy the claim that kids can throw unlimited innings, and neither does Mary Beth's orthopedist, who has treated her for a broken pitching elbow and rotator cuff tendinitis. But neither coach thought of removing these girls, and I think they would have had black eyes if they tried.

Scoreless eighth. In the ninth, Mary Beth got into the jam of all jams. She hit a batter ("No I didn't; it hit her bat," she said later, but the ump's vote was the only one that counted), and then walked her first batter of the game. Then, a perfectly placed bunt. Bases loaded, no outs. Tension on the Mounties' side. Glee on Cedar Grove's, whose players could smell their biggest win of the year. Next batter: Pitcher's best friend, a little pop to the first baseman. Next batter: Hard ground ball eight feet to first baseman Jess Giammella's right. She dived, speared the ball and, from her knees, sidearmed a throw home, where Sarfati waited with her right foot on the plate for the force. The ball was low and way outside. Sarf stretched, and stretched, and here came the go-ahead run, and Sarf scooped a one-hopper out of the dirt, almost doing a balance-beam split with

"I'm flattered that [Alabama] may have been interested in me, but it never really progressed, because we just never let it progress."

—Dolphins coach Nick Saban on Dec. 7, 2006

"I'm not going to be the Alabama coach."

—Saban on Dec. 21, 2006

"It took us a long time to get out of there, but we're happy to be here."

—Terry Saban, wife of new Alabama coach Nick, in Tuscaloosa on Jan. 3, 2007

"What I realized in the last two years is that we love college coaching."

—Nick Saban on Jan. 4, 2007

I think the Redskins were officially out of their minds in 2006 when they dealt two mid-round picks to San Francisco for wideout Brandon Lloyd. Over the course of a year, Washington traded for two receivers (Lloyd, Santana Moss) and signed two others (Antwaan Randle El, David Patten) who, with the exception of speed, fit the same profile (5' 10", 190). I'm not saying you have to have receivers of all shapes and sizes but maybe it would have been a good idea to get a taller, more physical receiver to play against some of the mooses at safety in the division, like Roy Williams?

two fibers of her right cleat touching the black of home plate. Time stopped. The ump went around to the side, stared at the foot, looked for the ball ... *and rang her up!* "*Outtttttt!*"

You think it's over? It ain't over. Now for Calcagno. No place to put her. Strike, outside corner. Ball, high. "Every pitch I throw now is a screwball," said Mary Beth, who just wants every ball to tail away from our county's Dot Richardson. Next pitch: *Ping!* Another hard grounder to short. Giannetti guns her down at first. We're out of it. Massive hugs on the Montclair side. The Cedar Grove coach, Rob Stern, looks up at the sky as if to ask, "Hey, God, you couldn't just give me one hit from the best hitter in New Jersey? C'mon!"

Sweeney was rolling. She had a 1-2-3 ninth. Mary Beth and Kaitlyn posted 1-2-3 10ths, and Mary Beth had officially pitched longer than in any other game in her life. In the 11th, Cedar Grove had a runner on second with one out, and our freshman second-baseman, Courtney Taylor, grabbed a looper and touched the second base bag for the double play. We went to the 12th. Uh-oh. Cedar Grove, with one out, picked up an infield single, followed by its second walk of the game, and a bunt single. Jammed again. *No más! No más!* We can't take it anymore. Mary Beth had their third hitter 1–2. Sarf set up outside. Mary Beth painted the black. Called strike three. Next kid: jammed inside on the first pitch. Pop to left.

I mean, does Mary Beth King have nine lives or what?

We got 'em 1-2-3 again in the 12th. Thirteen innings now. Thirteen. That's two games. Mary Beth was at 166 pitches. Lucky for her it was a three-batter inning.

Bottom 13. One out. Mary Beth (1 for 5, 2 K's to this point) up. Sweeney was on fire. She had retired 14 in a row with that nasty outside sinker.

"There was no way I could go out there and pitch any more," Mary Beth said later. "My arm was dead."

"Really?" I asked. "Would you have gone out there again?"

"Of course," she said. "What choice did I have?"

So she started thinking about her at bat. "Every time up, I'd taken the first strike," she said. "Kaitlyn's smart. She must have caught on, because every first or second pitch was a perfect strike, the kind of strike where you're watching the game and you say: 'I can't believe she didn't swing at that pitch!' So I figured, I'm swinging at the first pitch, wherever it is."

It was right over the heart of the plate.

Ping!

A few years ago when HBO dispatched me to interview Sen. John McCain in the Capitol on the subject of leadership, he raved for 40 minutes about Brett Favre and Ray Lewis.

Up the right-centerfield gap, splitting the out-fielders. Mary Beth steamed into third. A standup triple to open the inning.

Well, the bleachers shook and our bench exploded. Mary Beth just stood on third. A little pumped, but basically just catching her breath. I have often wondered this about her: Where does the cool come from? The reserve? Wherever it comes from, I'd like to patent it.

Now Meg Mylan, our third baseman and third hitter, stood in. Infield in. Kaitlyn threw, and Meg popped one just beyond the baseline between second and first. Their fielders sprinted for it. It ker-plunked into the clay. Mary Beth steamed home.

Ball game. Montclair, 3–2.

Two Cedar Grove gloves slammed to the ground. The Montclair side sounded like a jet engine. Mary Beth made a beeline for Meg and leaped into her arms. *"You the man!"* she yelled. Then the Montclair team caught up to the two heroines and pummeled them.

Two teams. Two pitchers. Three hours. Four hundred hoarse voices. One incredible bang-bang forceout at home.

One hundred batters. Dead even after 98. The 99th got a pitch six inches more to her liking than before. Six inches. The 100th locates a blooper perfectly. And that is how drama unfolds.

Dan Marino dressed up as Jay Fiedler on Halloween in 2002.

There is nothing like high school sports. Anywhere. Boys, girls, it doesn't matter. They play with the same ferocity. The joy for the winners is the same. The tears for the losers are as wet. You can't simulate these experiences as kids get ready to go out into the world. You think Kaitlyn Sweeney's going to be afraid the night before a big final at Penn State next year? She'll laugh at being afraid. She'll prepare the same way she prepared to be a great pitcher, and she'll win the test.

Fifteen minutes after the game, Mary Beth was pulling off her cleats. A Bazooka comic fell out of her shoe. "Here, Coach," she said, handing Palmieri the comic. Seems that before the game the coach had opened a piece of gum, liked what the fortune said, and told Mary Beth to hang on to it. After the game Palmieri was hanging on to the comic, her souvenir for the day. In exchange she handed Mary Beth the game ball.

The fortune read: "The ones who prepare are the lucky ones."

And that is my softball story for the year.

If you have any doubt that sports teach kids life lessons, remember the smarts and resilience and work ethic that these high school athletes put in. I am very bullish on the importance of high school sports. ●

Jolene at the Fairfield Inn front desk in Bourbonnais, Ill., is a great gal. I asked if there was some place to do my laundry in the hotel or nearby. "No, but I can do it for you," she said. "Just give me your stuff and I'll take care of it." I took $20 and handed to her and she said, "No! I could never take that!" Practically had to throw it at her. When I returned later that night after watching the Bears practice, there were four shirts hanging in my room, the rest of the clothes neatly folded, and a note from her, thanking me for the $20. Someday I expect to return to Bourbonnais and see Mayor Jolene in action.

My 2003
Super Bowl pick
(pregame):
"Raiders 17, Bucs
16. Bet the under."

*Tampa Bay
won 48–21. The
over/under was 46.*

More Things I Think I Think

The NFL's Best (And Worst)

Offering up my opinions on stadiums, airports, traditions, pet peeves and watering holes

I think these are my five favorite venues in the NFL:

1. LAMBEAU FIELD (GREEN BAY). The field is beautiful and history-filled, obviously. But I love the fact that strangers can walk through the parking lot before the game, meet total strangers, and within 90 seconds be deep into a brat and Leinenkugel. Coolest feature: The ceiling lighting in the Packers locker room is shaped like a football, complete with lit laces.

2. HEINZ FIELD (PITTSBURGH). As you walk into the place you just feel like you're going somewhere so, so important. And the place itself has no phonies, no one is there to be seen. The music is the same as it was at Three Rivers 30 years ago, as is the quality of football. All's that's missing: Myron Cope.

3. QWEST FIELD (SEATTLE). A pleasant surprise, I think because of the noise. I love fans who attend a game to love their team and hate the opposition, and it's surprising to see such a loud East Coast–type feel in the more civil Pacific Northwest. Plus, any place with espresso wafting through the concourses is good with me.

4. LP FIELD (NASHVILLE). I have no idea what LP means, or why there's a different name on this stadium every 15 or 20 minutes. I just know that the sight lines are terrific, the noise huge, and it's one of those places you love to visit because you can stay downtown, see a good game and never get in a car.

5. CLEVELAND BROWNS STADIUM. Downtown, walking distance from everywhere, players love the surface, both locker rooms are spacious and convenient to the field, wide concourses, all the creature comforts, Dawg Pound intact ... now all they need is a team to cheer for.

I think these are my five favorite U.S. airports:

1. SPOKANE INTERNATIONAL AIRPORT. Talk about going back in time. Moms with kids waiting to pick up dad off his business trip, running to hug him when he gets through security. People everywhere ... actually reading! Reading! Did you hear me? And reading real live books. Short walk to every gate, obviously.

2. SEA-TAC AIRPORT, *Seattle.* How about this? The top two airports in the country, both

My 2004 Super Bowl pick (preseason): "St. Louis 28, Buffalo 20."

Buffalo went 6–10 that season; St. Louis lost its first playoff game.

in the state of Washington. Just beyond the ticket counters are restaurants—with actual edible food—and an excellent, big bookstore. I'd estimate there are 452 coffee bars in the place, which doesn't hurt.

3. DENVER INTERNATIONAL AIRPORT. I'm going to overlook the fact that it's 35 minutes from downtown, which stinks. But the concourses are nice and big, and it's a good place to be stuck for a while. Try the Boulder Beer Taphouse, and order the red beer, whatever it is. Had four of those in a thunderstorm once.

4. MINNEAPOLIS-ST. PAUL INTERNATIONAL AIRPORT. One pet peeve: Approaching it on the local highway, the airport has huge signs for the Lindberg Terminal and the Humphrey Terminal. Well, how would anyone know which terminal houses which airlines if there's no sign saying, for instance, "Northwest is in the Lindberg Terminal?" Dumb. But beyond security is the nicest set of shops and both Starbucks and Caribou coffee shops. Good place to kill a few hours if you must.

5. PITTSBURGH INTERNATIONAL AIRPORT. Brilliantly designed, with stores and restaurants in a hub in the middle, with four convenient spokes housing all the gates, none more than a four- or five-minute walk from the hub. So

THANKS FOR THE MEMORIES—BOTH OF THEM.

—Sign in the end zone at Sun Devil Stadium during the final Cardinals game played on the Arizona State campus, on Dec. 24, 2005, after 18 profoundly lousy seasons there.

sad to see it now, with about 40% of the traffic and commerce that it was designed for because the city is struggling and the economy is too.

I think these are the five worst U.S. airports:

1. **JFK INTERNATIONAL AIRPORT,** *New York.* Inconvenient, too spread out, horribly designed. If you park in the wrong garage for the wrong airline, God help you. The Kennedy family should sue to get its good name back.

2. **LaGUARDIA AIRPORT,** *New York.* Dirty. I mean, how hard is it to keep a place semiclean? Plus the runways are short and scary.

3. **T.F. GREEN AIRPORT,** *Warwick, R.I.* For one reason and one reason only: security lines. If you've got a morning flight, and you're not there 90 minutes before your plane, don't even bother getting in line. I waited 75 minutes a couple of years ago, and figured it just must be a bad day. Nope. That's every day, according to my experience.

4. **KANSAS CITY INTERNATIONAL AIRPORT.** In a city as relatively rural as any, why put the airport a half-hour from downtown? And the gates are right next to the curbs, so you can't get out at one spot and hit all the gates; if your Delta flight is canceled and you have to find your way to Continental, you have to get on a shuttle bus, which for an airport this small is ridiculous.

I think guard Jamie Nails is two men! Or three! In December 1999 Nails was listed at 354 by the Bills. I will make this pronouncement right now: I am closer to a modeling contract with Abercrombie & Fitch than Nails was to 354. He last saw 354, I believe, in kindergarten.

Among the questions on the Giants' 480-question personality test given to all draft prospects: *Do you enjoy beating animals?* "And I wondered," said Oregon quarterback Joey Harrington, who took the test in 2002, "if you're a linebacker, should you say yes?"

5. DULLES INTERNATIONAL AIRPORT, *Northern Virginia.* Anyone figure out that silly toll road in and out of the place? Anyone understand why there are three airports around the D.C. beltway? Anyone figure out why you have to take a bus on stilts to get to most of the gates at this little city three hours outside Washington, D.C.?

I think these are my five favorite NFL traditions:

1. TEAMS GOING AWAY FOR TRAINING CAMP. I will bang the drum on this one forever. Teams are losing touch with their fans, and players need to be able to touch those who support them so well—not just those who pay for special access, or who are sons of advertisers. I see kids every year who will never forget close encounters with good-guy players on campuses around the country. Jake Delhomme's a gem to fans at the Panthers' camp at Wofford College. So is Ray Lewis with the Ravens at Western Maryland College, Tommie Harris of the Bears at Olivet Nazarene College and Jared Allen of the Vikings at Minnesota State in Mankato. That human touch is vital. Only 15 of 32 teams still go away to camp. It should be 32 of 32.

2. TAILGATING. A few years ago the Jets considered building a stadium in Manhattan, but the plan would have cut out all tailgating because of the lack of space. Fans would have figured out some way to drink and stuff themselves with charbroiled grub, but the sense of community would have been lost. I remember the International Harvester tailgate in Lambeau Field a few years back because, two hours before the game, they invited me in and filled me with two brats and the best Wisconsin cheddar from a huge cheese wheel. What more can you ask for in life?

3. THE TERRIBLE TOWEL. Actually, I love everything about Steelers football and tradition. But the towel, born of a Myron Cope idea in the '70s, symbolizes everything good about Steelers fandom. It's a simple hand towel—gold or white or black—still sold today, with all proceeds benefiting a school for the physically and mentally challenged. I have seen the Towel in Afghanistan and Kyrgyzstan, and it has been planted atop Mount Everest. And $7 for the most recognizable fan product in the NFL is pretty reasonable.

4. THE DAWG POUND. It's not as good as it used to be, because the tickets in the new Browns stadium are more expensive than in the old days at Cleveland Stadium. "But you still get pelted with those little bones," Hines Ward says. The little doggie treats, he means. Cool idea. Now if the Browns can just give these end-zone fans some reason other than anger to throw those bones.

"I'm not going to comment on the penalty situation. I'm not going to get fined on it. I'm not going to comment on it and that's it. I'm not commenting on it. I'm not commenting on the officiating. . . . Was it called? Yeah, it was called. And I'm not commenting on the call. You want to ask the guy who made the call what he saw, then go ask him. I'm not commenting on the officiating."

—Bill Belichick, not commenting six different times on the officiating, after the Patriots' 26–13 loss to Miami in October 2002.

Overheard on a Delta flight leaving Newark for Atlanta: "Hello, Jim? Bad news for you on this end. I never met up with Roseanne last night to make the final arrangements on that deal. Told her I'd meet her at this hotel in Newark at 6:30. I waited and waited and finally called her on her cell and said: 'Where are you? Snow holding you up?' She said, 'Where are you? I'm in the lobby of the hotel waiting for you.' I said, 'That's impossible. I'm in the lobby and I don't see you.' So we try to find each other and I realize she's not in this hotel. She's in a hotel in Newark, Delaware! Is that amazing? She got the wrong Newark!"

5. THE THURSDAY NIGHT OPENER. Can a tradition be just four or five years old? John Madden always said, rightfully, that the NFL didn't make its opening game special enough. Where was the bunting and the parade? By setting aside the Thursday night before the Sunday openers for the defending Super Bowl champ to open at home, the league has made the first game special and guaranteed itself a huge TV audience.

I think these are my five pet peeves with the NFL:

1. THE LEAGUE DOESN'T MAKE EACH TEAM STAND ON THE SIDELINES FOR THE NATIONAL ANTHEM. That's just wrong. Some teams do, some don't. In this era of cooperation between the league and the military, every player, before every game, should stand at attention for America's song.

2. PERSONAL SEAT LICENSES. I hate them. I wish the NFL took more of a stand against them or at least limited the amount that teams could charge. It's not fair that a Giants fan who has followed the team from Yankee Stadium to Shea Stadium to the Yale Bowl to Giants Stadium now has to pay a $20,000 PSL for his 40-yard-line seat.

3. FOUR PRESEASON GAMES. And not just because teams charge regular-season prices for them. They're a sham. Teams are much better off taking their bottom 40 players early in the pre-season and playing a couple of controlled scrimmages against nearby teams.

4. THE ENDLESS STREAM OF OFF-SEASON TRAINING SESSIONS, MINI-CAMPS AND MAXICAMPS THAT TEAMS KEEP EXPANDING EVERY YEAR. If a player's season ends in late January, for example, he has to start mandatory/voluntary training at his team's facility in mid-March. It continues weekly till around the Fourth of July. Then he's off for three weeks, and then training camp begins.

5. DRAFT PREP. Stupid, stupid, stupid. At the scouting combine last year, one G.M. was bemoaning the overkill of predraft work this way: "For a very marginal pick, like a sixth-rounder, we'll have four scouts see him in person, then we'll go to his pro day, and we might even have him in to visit us. We'll have his position coach study four or five games he played." All for a guy who likely will be a special-teamer at most. The New Orleans Saints had four draft picks last spring. For those four choices, the Saints paid a staff of 13 scouts and personnel people to spend nine months researching, and then the coaching staff dove in for the last four months. There is no good reason that the draft shouldn't be held two weeks after the scouting combine.

From 4-12-04: I know what San Diego G.M. A.J. Smith must be thinking right now. How can I not take Eli Manning with the first pick in the draft? This is the organization that six years ago missed out on Peyton Manning and took the bust of all time, Ryan Leaf. This is the franchise that 21 years ago didn't trade for John Elway because team officials thought the price was too high. So there is tremendous pressure on San Diego to make the right choice at quarterback when the draft kicks off. I am here to say the easy choice is Eli Manning. The right choice is Philip Rivers.

Thirtyish Man, a full four sheets to the wind, sitting two stools down at the Winking Lizard in downtown Cleveland one Saturday night around 10:30: "You a Browns fan?" Me, trying to watch Red Sox–Mariners: "No, not really." Thirtyish Man: "Ravens?" Me: "Nah. I like football, but I don't really root for one team." Thirtyish man: "You gotta like somebody!" Me: "No, I don't." Pause. Thirtyish man: "I don't believe you." No words were exchanged between the two Winking Lizard patrons after that.

I think these are the five best bars in the NFL:

1. NICKY'S LIONSHEAD TAVERN, *(Green Bay), De Pere, Wis.* You drink Spotted Cow ale and re-live the glory days. It's at Nicky's where an op-tometrist from La Crosse told me he dreamed of going shopping with Brett Favre. After a few Spotted Cows.

2. UNION HOTEL, *(Green Bay), De Pere, Wis.* Maybe I just drink all the time in Green Bay. I don't know. But this place opened in 1918, and you feel like it's where Lombardi went for his Friday night toddy with Marie. A great place to soak up Packer lore.

3. NEMO'S, *Detroit.* A long walk from Ford Field (there's shuttle service, however) this former Tiger Stadium hangout is a place straight out of the '50s, with covers from SI and Page Ones from local papers on big days displayed on the walls. Crowded. Fun. Loyal even in the bad times.

4. WINKING LIZARD TAVERN, *Cleveland.* Great fans here, good beer from everywhere, and lots of TV views. When you're in there, do not denigrate Rocky Colavito or Brian Sipe.

5. CLANCY'S, *New Orleans.* It's a little Creole res-taurant with a bar on Annunciation Street that you'll never find without a good cabbie. But if you want to feel like you're in the heart of a great city and talk to people who really know the Saints, go there and have a couple of pops.

Chemistry, Class with Mike Martz

The Rams coach built great game plans, but he also built his players' psyches and a solid reputation

I know that Mike Martz has been a tough guy to get along with for many in our business, but I like him. He's an original. There's so much imagination and emotion in him, and quite a bit of humanness. Once, when he knew his time in St. Louis was growing short after a spate of battles with the front office, he reached behind his desk and handed me a blue three-ring binder and said, "Take it." I began flipping through it. "A game plan," I said. Martz said he wouldn't need the complete offensive game plan from one of the Greatest Show on Turf games that he coached, and told me to take it. I've still got it.

There is a baby-changing station in the press box men's room at Invesco Field in Denver, home of the Broncos.

The paths of associate head coach Al Saunders and defensive tackle Jeff Zgonina crossed just outside head coach Mike Martz's office about noon on Saturday. Saunders is an offensive guy. Zgonina (pro-

One day I was walking on Park Avenue South between 25th and 26th streets in New York City when something very close to the Cigar Store Indian episode of *Seinfeld* happened to me. Remember that one? Jerry's on the sidewalk with Winona, the Native American woman he's trying to date, and Kramer goes by in a cab with a cigar-store Indian hanging out the window, and he yells, "Hey Jerry! Woo-woo-woo-woo-woo!" Well, some guy rolled down the rear window in the yellow cab he was riding in, stuck out his head, and yelled to me, "Hey Peter! *Eighteen and one! Eighteen and one!*"

nounced ska-NEE-nah), obviously, hangs with the defense. On NFL teams the offense and defense live in separate worlds maybe 70% of the time, on the practice fields and in meeting rooms. It is hard, then, for a coach and a player on opposite sides of the ball to be tight. Zgonina's father died of pancreatic cancer last week near Chicago, and this was the first time Saunders had seen the kid since he got back from the funeral.

"I'm so sorry about your dad," Saunders said.

"Thanks, Coach," Zgonina said.

And they hugged. Not a quickie, perfunctory hug, but a meaningful, slap-on-the-back, I-feel-for-you-kid embrace from a coach who, if he didn't share Zgonina's pain, was sure doing a good job faking it.

Which brings me to the point of this column: how to build chemistry and an old-fashioned team spirit these days among 53 fairly rich men. I saw that good feeling on Saturday in the Rams' locker room, this happy group shouting down a nonshowerer after a light practice, practically shaming him into cleanliness. Guffaws everywhere. I watched lots of Rams' offensive game tape on Friday and Saturday, and I noticed wide receiver Isaac Bruce dive-blocking his guts out on pass plays not intended for him; and I saw teammates thrilled and back-slapping when the fifth wideout, Tony Horne, caught a touchdown pass against the 49ers in Week 3. I know how much the locker room roots for Trent Green, who had his knee taken out 13 months earlier; Bruce is protective of him, sort of like a little brother. I heard corny stuff like this: I knew Ricky Proehl grew up a huge Giants fan in a family with Giants season tickets so I asked him if he'd like to run out of the tunnel in the Meadowlands just once wearing the blue and white before he retires. "It'd be great," he said, "but I want to retire a Ram. Mike's already talked to me about it."

That's Mike, as in head coach Martz, who has made it a point to be a psyche-builder as well as a game-plan builder. Case in point: He found out Zgonina's father was ill with cancer last summer. Martz invited Zgonina's dad to be on the sidelines during a preseason game, when he was still well enough to do so. He made Zgonina one of the captains for the game. Beaming father and son, just before the game, were photographed on the sidelines together. Zgonina told Martz on Monday that his dad had taken a turn for the worse, and Martz told him to go home, where he belonged, and not worry about practice this week—just try to make it back for Sunday's game. You think Zgonina won't go through a wall for this guy?

Corey Dillon's 50-yard run against the Jets on Nov. 12, 2006, was New England's first rush of 50 yards or more in this century.

Martz credits Dick Vermeil for worrying about chemistry and character when he drafted (though he ridiculously coddled a player he didn't draft, Lawrence Phillips) and signed free agents. "Dick did a great job setting the table for me," Martz said on a quiet afternoon behind his desk at Rams Park. "I'm the beneficiary of a great situation. You coach your whole life for a chance like this, to coach a team with this much talent. And what makes it so special is it's a team full of brothers. Kurt Warner, no ego. Isaac Bruce, you see him on the practice field talking to the managers and groundskeepers. Marshall Faulk, team guy. The stars are leaders and they lead in the right direction."

What does this mean on Sunday? No one knows. No one can quantify it. But when Martz disparages the Broncos for what he thinks is dirty blocking technique (and sends a tape of what he considers dirty plays to the league office), he's getting the guys in the trenches on his side. When he puts Horne and third tight end Jeff Robinson in the game to make catches at key times in big games, every guy down on the depth chart knows that Martz isn't blowing smoke about how this is a 53-man game, and that they'd all better be ready to play. We all know the Rams are winning now because they have the best offense that most of us have ever seen. Martz is trying to prolong the success by making sure

Early one Sunday morning in November 2000 a leashed dog exited the left elevator of the south elevator bank at the Seattle Westin, followed by a participant on his way to the Seattle Marathon. The dog left three steaming calling cards in the elevator. You just can't make this stuff up.

the atmosphere is so good around the team that if players have a chance to make more money in free agency (Torry Holt, Az Hakim, London Fletcher), they'd consider staying with the Rams for less, just to be a part of this touchy-feely greatness.

I'll believe that when I see it. But I'm starting to think that if it can be done, Martz has a shot to do it.

Postscript: After Sunday's 57–31 ho-hummer against San Diego, Martz choked up when he announced the awarding of the game balls. One to Zgonina. One to Green, who got KO'd by the Chargers in the 1999 preseason and on Sunday came back to throw a touchdown pass on his first drive in a real game since. Walking out of the press conference with Martz, I said, "You got a little emotional in there."

"Had to," Martz said, biting his lower lip. "Jeff's like a son to me. I love Trent. This team loves Trent. . . . "

Then for a minute he couldn't say anything else.

Once, Martz invited me to St. Louis for a charity golf tournament. After the round of golf, everyone adjourned to Martz's suburban house. Stan Musial and Whitey Herzog were there, and Martz said to me, "How incredible is this! Stan Musial's in my kitchen! How lucky can a guy be!"

In March 2003 the New York *Daily News* reported that *Playboy* was considering a "Women of Starbucks" pictorial for an upcoming issue. Wow. Things might be getting a little frothy in MMQB when that happens.

MMQB Classic September 24, 2001

Tears and Then Cheers

In the wake of 9/11 we learned a lot about resiliency, pulling together and the importance of pro football

You felt the emotion of 9/11 everywhere in the country, certainly. But living in the shadow of the flattened towers, our family felt it daily, hourly.

The memory I'll never forget: Before the second tower fell, I couldn't watch TV anymore without doing something. I got into my car in Montclair, N.J., and drove to nearby West Orange, to the Blood Center of New Jersey. Recall that late in the morning after the towers got hit, we all still thought that there would be thousands of injured survivors.

When I got to the neighborhood with the blood bank, I almost started bawling. For nearly the length of a full block, a line of people stretched outside the building, all waiting patiently to donate.

I admit it: I cried yesterday.

Not in a weeping way. In a two-tears-reaching-the-upper-cheek way. Some Giants did, too. As I walked off the field with New York linebacker/

"Injury report for the Patriots. . . . Long-snapper Mike Bartrum has a broken arm . . . Will return."

—Metrodome press box P.A. announcer Kurt Mayer, in the third quarter of the New England–Minnesota game, Nov. 2, 1997.

preacher/leader Micheal Barrow, I could see the emotion all over his face. "This for the firemen and the policemen," he told me above the din of the Arrowhead speakers after the Giants won for a city, 13–3. "We dedicated this game to them. We're dedicating this season to them."

This has been an emotional time for me, living, as I do in New Jersey, 15 miles from Ground Zero. And for most of you, I'm sure. I can't read the paper much anymore. It's just too much. For the first four or five days of the disaster, I sat at the kitchen table for two hours in the morning, devouring every word of *The New York Times*. (And, by the way, this great, great newspaper will need a U-Haul to carry all the Pulitzers it's going to win for its thorough, meaningful and touching coverage of the disaster. Just terrific.) But I started to come out of it last Tuesday. My daughter Mary Beth, who has become quite a little patriot in her own way, and I went in search of 100 American flag patches to affix to the front of the Montclair High field hockey team jerseys in time for the resumption of play on Friday. All the suppliers in New Jersey were back-ordering the things—a buddy of mine had four complete high school football teams on hold—and so we had to widen the scope. A family friend found a place in New York City's garment district with

In October 2006 the complete message on Chad Johnson's cellphone voice-mail greeting was "Yeah."

the flags, so we drove in and picked them up. Neat scene. El-cheapo flags on every street corner, sold by loud people in 89 different dialects. "I love America," Mary Beth said for no particular reason, and for every particular reason, as we walked back to the car. First she had to find an "I Love New York" T-shirt, with a heart in place of the word *love*, just because she wanted to show she loved the place.

Then, on Tuesday night, humble SI Olympics beatman Brian Cazeneuve, the Mother Teresa of sportswriters and chief of our World Trade Center volunteer crew, arranged for me to join him at the New York Waterways ferry building, about three miles from the attack site on the western edge of Manhattan. Walking from the parking garage to the ferry building, a football fan noticed me and asked what would become of the playoffs. Wow, I thought; people are getting back into it. The building was serving as one of the waystations for supply organization. Boxes of all different things—gloves, work boots, foodstuffs, batteries, bottled water, flashlights—were arriving from all over the country, and busy beavers were sorting them around the clock to send to crews on the scene. For an hour I assembled flashlights. For four hours I paired cotton glove liners in big boxes with construction gloves. All donated. One

On StubHub, a single seat to the final game at old Yankee Stadium, lower level, between the dugout and home plate, was selling for $12,348.

package of assorted gloves came from a family from Yardley, Pa., the Elliotts. I know that because they included a note with "God Bless You" written on the envelope.

One of the volunteers, a construction worker from Chicago, told me he watched the TV coverage of the disaster for two nights after work. The third night, he said, he couldn't watch it anymore. He went to the bus terminal in Chicago and bought a ticket for New York. Arriving at the bus station in Manhattan at 10 p.m. the Friday after the attack, he asked a cop, "Where do you go to volunteer?" This was his fifth night working, and he wasn't planning on leaving anytime soon. Another volunteer drove from Miami the night of the disaster; when I commented on the almost unfathomable number of boxes of boots on the premises, he told me: "They'll need them all, and then some. Yesterday we sent 2,500 pair down to the site. Some of those guys are working on top of fires, and their soles just melt off."

Another woman, Cris Carnicelli, from Jackson Heights in Queens, is the girlfriend of a city firefighter who survived. She had volunteered every day. In the very wee hours, she pulled out some mementos and placed them on the floor of the Waterways building, in between the piles of gloves and flashlights and Kellogg's breakfast

From 11-24-97: If Bill Tobin stays the personnel-picker in Indianapolis and the Colts select first, I wouldn't be a bit surprised if they take Andre Wadsworth and let Paul Justin and Jim Harbaugh battle it out at QB next summer in camp.

Yeah, right. The Colts picked Peyton Manning.

I think Ron Dixon did the silliest thing I've seen in a long time, removing a glove after his 97-yard kickoff return for a touchdown and slapping the CBS camera during a playoff game in January 2001. I mean, what gets in the head of these people? What planet are you from when, at the most gleeful moment of your life you remove a glove and slap a national TV camera? Did the camera challenge him to a duel?

bars. Upper Moreland High School in Willow Grove, Pa., sent a huge paper flag, signed by the Class of 2002, in its care package. A Holy Bible came in a supply box sent from "friends in Memphis, Tenn." The inscription read: "To the courageous firemen and police officers . . . We're praying for you and your families during this terrible tragedy. Sept. 15, 2001. God bless you." Beneath was a smiley face.

Carnicelli, 31, a freelance editor in her other life, had seen and heard some bad things, gruesome things, from the firemen and guardsmen who'd come up from the disaster site. They will not be repeated here. But she knows these Stephen King–like bad things will haunt her at some point in the future. She knows she might be on a shrink's couch, for an extended run, someday soon. I asked her why she was here to help, day after day.

"I have to be here," she said. "It's the right thing to do. And it helps me heal."

I left there that night, a week after the world changed, about 2:40 a.m., feeling the best I'd felt in a week. People were banding together. People were uniting. People, a lot of them, were doing anything they could to help. Dropping $50 at Home Depots all over the country, boxing up the supplies and sending them to New York. Leaving their jobs, leaving their families. They wanted nothing, other than an answer to the question: "What can I do to help?"

My wife, Ann, who will hate being written about (she is not the publicity-seeking type), then came up with the Idea of the Week. New York's mayor Giuliani wants people to fill the streets and restaurants of the city, she had heard. Why not get a group from Montclair together Friday night and drive into the city and eat and drink heavily? Terrific, I said. I wanted to call the night, "Fight Terrorism . . . Eat Well." We settled on "Support New York City!" We corralled 16 people and car-pooled into loud and friendly Carmine's, a family-style Italian place, on 44th, just down the street from where *The Producers* is playing. And let me just say this about the city: It was packed. Couples walking arm in arm. Moms with strollers. Women in theater-wear. Jumping joints with the Mets and Braves on the bar TVs. Our table, with friends ranging from five years of age to 55, passed around the Italian salad, the cold antipasto, the garlic bread, the penne with marinara, the penne with meatballs, the lemon chicken, the salmon oreganato. (Quite a sacrifice, I must say. But we all have to do something for the cause.)

Early in the dinner, the long table to our right was filled by 15 Buffalo firefighters and cops. We bought them a round of drinks—only one, be-

A few years ago my wife and I took the train up to Boston on vacation for a couple of days. There was a guy in the seat in front of us conducting a business meeting for all the coach car to hear. This guy was not yelling, but he was making no attempt to hide anything he was saying. He had his ballpark voice on, a voice as loud as one you'd use to talk at a crowded ballpark during a game. I wish the people conducting private business in public would shut up and realize that those of us who don't conduct private business in public would like them to stuff a sock in it.

cause, as it turns out, they were returning for night duty at Ground Zero at 11—and they sent us a real Buffalo police patch in return. Mary Beth and her friend Steffi were closest to them and got the scoop. These men were earning nothing for their work. And they were taking vacation time and comp time from their jobs to do it. Why? "Because," one of them said, "people were in need."

The cops and firefighters rose to leave just after 10. As they filed by, someone at our table began to clap. Then we all began clapping. Then the next table began clapping. And the next. And soon, Carmine's was filled with whistling and clapping and hurrahs and backslaps, deafeningly so, and these humble men waved and bit their lips and looked at the floor as they walked out, emotionally stunned at the outburst. I looked back at our table and two of the women were dabbing at their eyes.

"Best idea you ever had," I told Ann.

Newark Airport looked relatively abandoned when I arrived Saturday at about 10 for an 11:30 a.m. flight to Kansas City. Armed U.S. marshals, in uniform, patrolled the Continental terminal, as did New Jersey state police; Continental gate agents, who for some reason I assume are more diligent about checking for weapons, helped man the metal detectors and X-ray machines. Michael Strahan's wife, Jean, was waiting for the flight to board

"Glad you came to New York. And my son Zack's got a great middle name."

—Text message from Browns coach Eric Mangini, formerly the Jets' head man, to Brett Favre on Favre's retirement day in February 2009. Zack Brett Mangini was born on Oct. 10, 2008, Favre's 39th birthday.

when I got to the gate. Jean was a bit jittery about flying and felt better when she realized that someone she knew was coming along. I told her nothing untoward was going to happen on this flight or any other, which is something I truly believe.

Nothing did. And then the Giants went out and played a victorious, inspiring sort of snoozer. I don't recall a locker room where the players looked as fatigued. This is what mental and physical stress does to people. But it was a happy kind of tired. I asked Michael Strahan what he would take away from this game.

"After the tragedy of last week," he said, "it was tough for me to figure out, 'What is our purpose? Why are we playing football?' Then we went down to Ground Zero and people kept telling us they needed us to play. And so we came in here playing for the firefighters, the police, the EMS workers, for everybody. For a city."

It was corny, what Strahan said next, but it didn't sound that way on Sunday. Not these days.

"I'm proud to be a football player today," he said. "And I'm proud to be an American."

It's nine years later, and I still remember what I thought when I wrote those words in the Westin Crown Plaza Hotel in downtown Kansas City:

So am I. ●

Donovan McNabb's mother, Wilma, is a registered nurse. In June 2003 McNabb married Raquel Nurse.

PETER KING's FOOTBALL

RISING SON
Yakima, Wash.
p. 224

JOE COLLEGE
Madison, Wis.
p. 245

ROAD TRIP
Brady, Neb.
p. 214

MEET THE XFL
Las Vegas
p. 232

ENDGAME
Englewood, Colo.
p. 238

HOMECOMIN
Mumford, Texas
p. 230

FEEDBACK
Santa Clara, Calif.
p. 228

QUITTIN' TIME
Palm Desert, Calif.
p. 212

THE MAVERICK
San Antonio
p. 240

AMERICA

Looking back on 20 memorable stops from my two decades on the NFL beat for SPORTS ILLUSTRATED

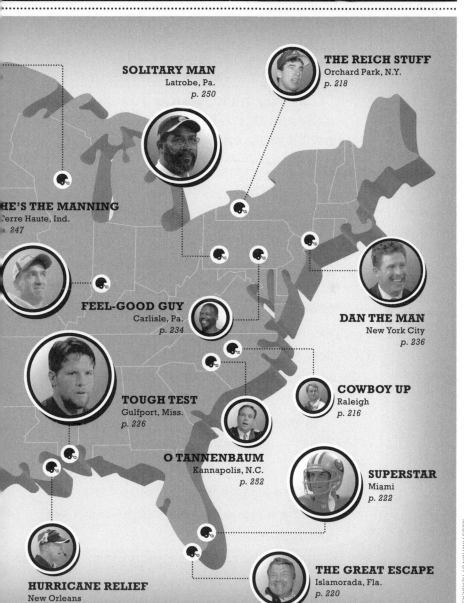

THE REICH STUFF
Orchard Park, N.Y.
p. 218

SOLITARY MAN
Latrobe, Pa.
p. 250

HE'S THE MANNING
Terre Haute, Ind.
247

FEEL-GOOD GUY
Carlisle, Pa.
p. 234

DAN THE MAN
New York City
p. 236

TOUGH TEST
Gulfport, Miss.
p. 226

COWBOY UP
Raleigh
p. 216

O TANNENBAUM
Kannapolis, N.C.
p. 252

SUPERSTAR
Miami
p. 222

HURRICANE RELIEF
New Orleans
p. 242

THE GREAT ESCAPE
Islamorada, Fla.
p. 220

ILLUSTRATION BY HEADCASE DESIGN

Peter King's Football America

Map Quest

From Yakima to Islamorada, Rozelle to Reich, these are the stories behind my 20 most unforgettable stories

Pete Rozelle

QUITTIN' TIME

Palm Desert, Calif. — March 1989

I am in a swanky hotel in the Southern California desert, waiting for an afternoon press conference at the annual NFL meetings. I have resisted the urge to go the California Angels afternoon exhibition game in Palm Springs. When I have the pelts on the wall that my friend/mentor Will McDonough does, I'll skip a press conference at the league meetings to see baseball in the blazing sun, but that's a few years down the road, at least.

At these meetings the commissioner usually speaks at the opening and the closing, and here we were, near the end, on a Wednesday afternoon, and the man who had been commissioner since I was four walked into the room and said he was quitting.

Hell. Breaks. Loose.

"I decided in October," Rozelle says, "but I didn't want to become a lame-duck commissioner. It's just a matter of wanting to enjoy my free time.

I asked myself, 'Is that all there is to life—work, die and never experience retirement?'"

Rozelle looks old. He is 63. Tanned, attentive, still engaged in everything. But that day I remember interviewing him in his New York office a couple of years earlier, and every third or fourth sentence came back to something litigious. He just couldn't take it anymore. Two strikes in his last seven years, the civil war with Al Davis, nobody ever happy despite being a part of the most successful sports league in America. Let it be someone else's problem.

And that day, six people seemed to be in control of the future of the NFL: Rozelle, who would lord over the game until a successor was found; influential owners Wellington Mara and Lamar Hunt, who would lead the search for a new commissioner; and prime candidates Tex Schramm, Jim Finks and Jack Kemp.

Writing those words now, I realize how full of change the league has been over the last 20 years. All six of those men are dead.

On that day in Palm Desert, Jerry Jones's ownership of the Cowboys was one month old. Daniel Snyder, 23, was running a travel business out of his parents' home near Washington, D.C. Roger Goodell was an unknown bureaucrat in the league office, the assistant to the president of

> Rozelle just couldn't take it anymore. Two strikes in his last seven years, the civil war with Al Davis, nobody ever happy despite being a part of the most successful sports league in America. Let it be someone else's problem.

the American Football Conference. Brett Favre was a sophomore at Southern Miss, on no team's radar screen as a pro prospect. Tom Brady was 11. I'm guessing he was riding his bike home from sixth grade around the time Rozelle shocked the world with his announcement.

I'm reminded of something Bill Parcells said once. "We're all part-timers in this game. When we're done, the game will spit us out, and it'll be bigger than ever." He's right. The National Football League is a freight train roaring down the tracks. And no one is bigger than the game.

ROAD TRIP
Brady, Neb. — November 1990

I am on John Madden's bus, his Hyatt suite on wheels, in the middle of the United States. It's late in the afternoon of Day Two of a trip from Madden's home outside San Francisco to his apartment at the Dakota in New York. He's got the Giants and Cowboys in New Jersey on Sunday.

There are two drivers on the bus, Willie Yarbrough and Dave Hahn. They take turns sleeping and driving and staring out the window. Then there's Madden's son Joe, and a neighbor from California who, like me, is taking a joyride. The first third of the bus is seating, with two benches facing each other. The middle of the bus has a bathroom

John Madden

with a rudimentary shower and a kitchen. The rear third, or maybe rear 40%, is Madden's bedroom, with a king-size bed, big TV and VCR.

I provided some comic relief on the bus. At least I think it was funny. Maybe the laughter was uneasy, and Madden retired to his bed at night, thinking, "Why'd we take this greenhorn idiot on the trip with us?" On Day One of the trip, I opened a large bottle of water, I think a 33.8-ounce bottle, took a few sips, put it in one of the beverage holders at the end of the benches, and got up and walked to the middle of the bus.

"Whoa! Whoa! Whoa! Hold on!" Madden yelled. "Bottle rule!"

Huh?

"We've got one big rule on the bus," Madden told me. "You start a bottle of water, you finish it."

That's a big bottle of water. On the Madden bus, you better either be very thirsty or love hydration.

Madden is at his best late at night. The biff-bam-boom stuff hides in the darkness, and he just talks. There's the trademark Madden enthusiasm and interest, but it's quiet. He's a night owl, preferring to watch game tape alone when he and the driver might be the only two people awake on the bus. I doubt much has changed over the years.

The most interesting moment of the trip came on I-80, most of the way across Nebraska, when

Madden is at his best late at night. The biff-bam-boom stuff hides in the darkness, and he just talks. There's the trademark Madden enthusiasm and interest, but it's quiet.

we stumbled on a strange animal farm. "Pull over," Madden said. We stopped on the side of the road and got out of the bus. Strange. In a two-acre holding pen were 30 or 40 animals of different sorts, including what appeared to be a cross-bred deer/llama and other crossbred animals that looked like llamas with bizarrely swollen necks.

"He looks like he's on steroids," says Madden.

As we walked back to the bus, I say to Madden, "You see a lot of weird things driving cross-country."

"See how boring it is to fly?" he says. "I love this stuff."

Butch Davis

COWBOY UP

Raleigh — March 1991

I am on the campus of N.C. State, with a crew of six Dallas Cowboys coaches, investigating the Wolf-pack's crop of draft-eligible players. I'm a fly on the wall—and on the airplane wing—observing the new way of scouting. Only one team in the NFL (Cincinnati) uses its assistants as much as the Cowboys do. But Dallas applies a unique brand of scouting science. A smarter one, if you ask me. Most of the Dallas coaches were in college football one, two or three years ago; the Cincinnati coaches are veteran pro guys who do the same job as normal scouts. The Dallas coaches are friends with a lot of the college coaches they're visiting, and so they trust them to give up the real dirt.

We left the previous morning at 6 for Knoxville from Dallas on Jerry One, owner Jerry Jones's plane, and the coaches spent the day grilling the staff of the nine-win Vols. Last night the coaches drank and sang at the home of coach Johnny Majors, an old friend of Cowboys coach Jimmy Johnson's. Special-teams coach Joe Avezzano sang a country song—exceptionally well—sometime around 1, and with a 6 a.m. flight, I'd have thought the fellows would have wanted to sleep. Well, at 3 they'd sleep for a couple of hours, but there was too much fun to be had. Johnson always wanted it that way. After today it would be on to Notre Dame, and then to Michigan State.

What I really wanted to know was how this drinking and schmoozing and film-watching helped the Cowboys on draft day. And this afternoon I found out.

In the football offices this morning, defensive line coach Butch Davis noticed that a top prospect, Mike Jones, was consistently taking plays off, even taking full series off, in big games. Something smelled rotten. Davis went around to all the defensive coaches, but he couldn't find the one aide who knew Jones well. For some reason that aide had the day off. But Davis found out

The Dallas coaches are friends with a lot of the college coaches they're visiting, and so they trust them to give up the real dirt.

where he lived. He went to his house. He found the guy. He asked what the deal was with Mike Jones taking all these plays off.

"I don't know if he's tough enough," the aide said.

Scratch that player off the Dallas draft list.

The plane waited for Davis at the Raleigh airport. When he boarded and told everyone what he had learned, the coaches burst out in applause.

Johnson, sitting across the aisle from me, looked over. "Now you know why we do it this way," he said, and laughed his triumphant Johnson laugh. "Now we won't waste a draft pick."

Two Super Bowls later, we found out Johnson was right about a lot of things.

Frank Reich

THE REICH STUFF

Orchard Park, N.Y. — January 1993

I am standing in the Buffalo locker room 90 minutes after one of the most stunning football games ever played. Buffalo 41, Houston 38, after the score had been Houston 35, Buffalo 3 with 28 minutes left. There is one player left in the locker room, the man who never, ever, ever will have a day like this in his chosen sport again.

"Can you bring Linda in?" Frank Reich says to one of the equipment guys.

Reich's wife is ushered into the room, and she

walks very fast over to him, and he to her, and he lifts her off the ground for 10, 12, maybe 15 seconds as they both laugh. I get choked up. I'm thinking, God, this looks just like one of those husband-comes-home-from-war pictures!

Funny thing about this game. Before kickoff, an in-studio guest on the NBC pregame show, Boomer Esiason, had some interesting things to say about his former Maryland teammate, Reich, who was starting for the injured Jim Kelly. "Watch out for Frank today," Esiason said. "I remember a game in college when he was down 31–0 to Miami, and he led the Terps back to win. So he's not going to be afraid of a big game."

Amazing. Reich brought a college team back from 31 points down to win. And now he'd brought a pro team back from 32 points down to win.

"There is only one way to play a game like this," he says, once he'd put his wife back on earth. "One play at a time. Anything other than that, and you'll think, 'It's impossible to come back from a deficit like this.' So that's all I did."

One play at a time, in the best game I ever saw. It's interesting. Every time I see Reich, I think of this game, and I want to say something about it. Reich would be polite about it, and he'd exult about it. But most players don't want to live in yesterday, and most players get sick of being

Amazing. Reich brought a college team back from 31 points down to win. And now he'd brought a pro team back from 32 points down to win.

known for one thing. Reich's a good guy, a really solid family man. And he's not going to live like the *Glory Days* pitcher that Bruce Springsteen sung about. I do think, though, that if you see him one day and you remind him of the time he lifted his wife off the ground in the locker room after the biggest win of his life . . . I think that'll make him stop and smile.

THE GREAT ESCAPE

Islamorada, Fla. — July 1994

Jimmy Johnson

I am in Woody's Saloon, in the place where Parrotheads go to disappear, the town of Islamorada in the Florida Keys. Midsummer. Really, really hot. So humid it feels like fish are swimming by you in mid-air.

Woody's Saloon is the place where Jimmy Johnson goes fishing for little green bottles—Heinekens (since replaced by Heineken Lights in Johnson's svelte new world)—and where he goes to listen to his favorite band, Big Dick and the Extenders. Tonight it's a karaoke night, and I am here with the recently unemployed Dallas Cowboys coach and his girlfriend, Rhonda Rookmaaker.

And I do something I'm not particularly proud of. After much cajoling, I join Johnson on stage and sing *Help Me Rhonda*. Well, "sing" is being generous; "mangle" is more accurate. You never know what's going to happen on a night out with Jimmy Johnson. Then Johnson does worse with *My Girl*, by the Temptations, during which one bar patron shouts: "Keep your day job, Jimmy!"

This *is* his day job. Four months after his famous dustup and divorce with Cowboys owner Jerry Jones (remember when a well-lubricated Jones thundered that "500 guys could coach this team?"), I encounter a man with a well-tanned hide doing everything he can to not think about football. He doesn't get a newspaper. He doesn't watch sports on TV. He doesn't gossip with friends around college or pro football. His is *out*, with a capital *O*.

"People come down here to get away from civilization, and they accomplish their goal," he says at the table. "That's not all bad. The question is: Once you get here, do you ever want to return? I mean, do you think I care what the practice schedule is at camp right now? You think I ever will?"

I remember a few months earlier, after the Cowboys won their second Super Bowl under Johnson, talking to him about how if he won another one or two of these things, he could make history. And he laughed. History, he said, held no interest for him. And tonight, in this bar, he scoffed at the idea of going back to the game so

Four months after his famous dustup and divorce with Cowboys owner Jerry Jones, I encounter a man with a well-tanned hide doing everything he can to not think about football.

that he could build a résumé to be known as one of the best coaches ever.

"I don't live for history," he says. "I live for the moment. If I go to another team ... we'll be the best team, and we'll win that third Super Bowl. If it doesn't happen, I'll be right here. And either way I'll be happier than ever."

Steve Young

SUPERSTAR

Miami — January 1995

I am with the Steve Young media conga line in the end zone at Joe Robbie Stadium, maybe 90 minutes after the biggest football game of his life, the 49–26 rout of the Chargers, in which he finally proved he could do what superhero Joe Montana did so often—shred a team in the Super Bowl. After he threw for a Super Bowl–record six touchdowns, Young did 24 interviews on the field and in the locker room, taking about 85 minutes. My job is to shadow Young during the entire postgame thing, and at one point, he looks at me, pale, and says, "You think you can find me something, anything, to eat and drink?" And so I go back underneath the stands and find four sugar cookies, two bottles of Gatorade and an apple. After he does his last live shot, he devours everything I've brought. The Gatorade takes approximately 2.7 seconds to go down. Both bottles.

So we—agent Leigh Steinberg, me, Young and a friend from college—get into a white limo for the ride back to the Airport Hilton, where the Niners were staying. Young still looks woozy.

"Feel awful," he says, and, as the car exits the parking lot, he proceeds to vomit all over Steinberg's shoes.

"Well," says Steinberg, "I'll never wash that shoe again."

Still so sick is Young back at the hotel suite—cramping, wretching, clearly dehydrated—that the Miami-Dade rescue squad is called. Two IVs are stuck in his arms, and he lies on his bed, receiving guests, 44 in all, well into the night.

Weakly, at one point, he musters this up, with a big grin: "Is this great or what? I mean, I haven't thrown six touchdown passes in a game in my life, and I throw six in the Super Bowl! Unbelievable."

Right then, someone yells, "Joe Who?"

And Young looks like he got punched in the gut. "No, no, no, don't do that," he says, brushing off the tiffs he had with the San Francisco legend. "Don't worry about that. That's the past. Let's talk about the future."

It turned out to be the only Super Bowl that Young would win. He barely got to enjoy it. But I've never seen anyone happier after winning one.

It turned out to be the only Super Bowl that Young would win. He barely got to enjoy it. But I've never seen anyone happier after winning one.

Drew Bledsoe

RISING SON

Yakima, Wash. — June 1995

I am at the home of Mac and Barbara Bledsoe, hard by acres and acres of apple orchards in central Washington. Driving here from Seattle was a gas. I love seeing the U.S., especially places like this town with the dads jogging behind four-year-olds learning to bike-ride, and the local park, with an older man reading a book on a bench on a summer day. Here at the modest Bledsoe home, there are family photos and trophies and footballs commemorating great games, and one of the first things I notice is the poem behind the dinner table.

> *One hundred years from now it will not matter*
> *What kind of car I drove*
> *What kind of house I lived in*
> *How much money I had in my bank account.*
> *Nor what my clothes looked like.*
> *But the world may be a little better*
> *Because I was important in the life of a child.*

What parents! Mac is a motivational speaker as well as a high school coach, and you have to be around him for about three minutes to see why Drew Bledsoe combined a que-sera-sera thing with a competitive streak. I'm sitting with the parents, and Mac says that if Drew had lived up to his expectations, the boy would have grown up to be a tight end at Montana. "But he knew what he wanted," Mac says. Like, being the current wunder-kind quarterback of the National Football League.

"Mac talks to hundreds and hundreds of peo-ple every year on parenting and self-esteem for children," Barbara says. "Not everyone buys into it. Drew bought in, totally. It got to the point where I'd be doing his laundry when Drew was in high school, and I'd find little notes in his pants pockets. They'd say things like, 'I hustle on every play,' and 'I make extra effort on every play,' and 'I live by team rules,' and 'I'm the first on the field and the last to leave.'"

Says Mac, "I believe in coaching and teaching, kids have to find their own way. Kids win. Coaches don't. I'm not positive about this stat, but in the 10 NCAA championship games coached by John Wooden, he called a timeout only once late in a game. His wizardry was during the week. Then he let his kids play."

Interesting, I said; now he's got Bill Parcells in his grill every Sunday. And Parcells doesn't sub-scribe to the let-the-kids-play-and-they'll-be-fine school of coaching. I ask Barbara how she feels when she sees Parcells on TV biting her son's tal-ented head off.

"I don't like it," she says. "That's not going to help Drew perform better."

When I go back East, I relay that statement

> "Mac talks to hundreds and hundreds of people every year on parenting and self-esteem for children," Barbara says. "Not everyone buys into it. Drew bought in, totally."

to Parcells. He neither frowns nor smiles. But it takes him less than a second to respond.

"Tell her not to watch the games."

TOUGH TEST

Brett Favre

Gulfport, Miss. — May 1996

I am on a golf cart with Deanna Tynes, the fiancée of Brett Favre. It is a beautiful, hot, muggy day in southern Mississippi at the Windance Country Club outside Gulfport. We are sitting under a shade tree by the 18th green.

Tynes is crying.

We're at the Brett Favre Celebrity Golf Tournament; only Brett Favre is not here. A day earlier he entered drug rehab in Topeka, Kans., and because the show must go on, he spent hours on the phone with the players and people expected to show up to make this first tournament a success. I'd been invited—remember, this was in the pre-Favre-as-legend days, and I was probably the only national media person who knew Favre more than in passing—and the guests were more B-list than A. He called me before I was to fly to Mississippi, and he talked about how he was going into rehab for a Vicodin addiction the next day, and his problem was so severe in the eyes of the NFL that the league wouldn't let him put off his admission into the clinic for three days while he raised money for his charity. He hoped I'd still attend the event and, along with the other golfers, muddle along without him. Weird, of course, but no one canceled.

And one of the things Favre said that night in a 40-minute confession/soul-cleansing/folk-storytelling session is something I'll remember as long as I do this job. "I'm 26 years old, I just threw 38 TD passes in one year, and I'm the NFL MVP," he said, his voice sounding sullen. "People look at me and say, 'I'd love to be that guy.' But if they knew what it took to be that guy, they wouldn't love to be him, I can guarantee you that. I'm entering a treatment center tomorrow. Would they love that?"

Tynes is tough as nails. She was then, and she still is. I have tremendous admiration for how she stuck with Favre during his cad days, and this, right here, right now, would be a real test of their relationship.

Now she dabs her eyes and looks out onto the golf course on a glorious Southern day. "A couple of years ago Brett told me he wanted to be the best quarterback in the NFL," she says. "He committed himself to do it, and he did it. He'll commit himself to this. He knows his career and his life are at stake."

It's days like this, in the epicenter of the biggest story in sports, that you get into this business for.

> "People look at me and say, 'I'd love to be that guy,'" Favre says. "But if they knew what it took to be that guy, they wouldn't love to be him, I can guarantee you that."

Kevin Gogan

FEEDBACK

Santa Clara, Calif. — September 1997

I have just entered the San Francisco 49ers' locker room on a Friday afternoon, after practice, and before I can make my way to the first player's locker, guard Kevin Gogan sees me. And explodes.

"Journeyman! . . . Journeyman!!!" Gogan screams, walking toward me. "How the #$%& can you call me a journeyman! What the #$%& is your problem!"

For a minute, I can't remember what in the world he's talking about. But I know that when I've ever had a livid 335-pound man walking toward me with a menacing glare, my powers of memory improve quickly.

A couple of months earlier I had written a profile of Steve Young. In it he bemoaned how unaggressive the 49ers had been in improving an aging team, and I'd referred to Gogan, one of the off-season additions, as a journeyman. Which, when you're on your third team in five years, is quite an apt term. (As it turned out, Gogan's career would end with his being on five teams in his final eight NFL seasons.)

Anyway, I fruitlessly try to explain the meaning. Too bad I didn't have my pocket dictionary with me, the one describing *journeyman* as a "qualified artisan." But Gogan stays in my face, yelling for maybe 45 seconds, and I let him vent, and then I try to go about my business, interviewing players, and as I go to a few lockers, different players scream "*journeyman!*" and Gogan steams. I won't get much interviewing done on this day.

The point is that negative reaction to something you've written is just part of the job of being a sportswriter, and if you can't deal with it, then don't go into the locker room.

The next time I saw Gogan—I forget; either later that year or the next—he was friendly, smiling. He had lit into me, and it was over. I've had other guys over the years who never forgot a criticism. Like Deion Sanders, who was finished when he signed with the Redskins, and I pointed out what a stupid signing and a waste of money it was—all true. But Sanders didn't like it, and we haven't spoken since.

I like a good duel with a player or owner who will disagree with you and not take it so personally that he'll hold it against you, right or wrong, forever. Like Gogan. And Jerry Jones. In August 2006 I said on NBC's *Football Night in America* that the Cowboys would seriously consider replacing Drew Bledsoe with Tony Romo sometime early in the season. On his radio show the next day, Jones said my report was "made up, with no substance." And Romo was the starter by Octo-

> The point is that negative reaction is just part of the job of being a sportswriter, and if you can't deal with it, then don't go into locker rooms.

ber. I've written a few things over the years that
Jones could say (and I'm sure has said), "King's
so wrong on that one." Part of the game. If you're
going to dish it out, you've got to be able to take it.

HOMECOMING

Mumford, Texas — February 1998

John Randle

I am with the meanest, strangest, Tasmanian devil
of a player in the NFL, Minnesota defensive tackle
John Randle, and he is blinking back tears, standing outside a wooden box with a corrugated metal
roof, maybe 400 square feet in size, with a strong
wind whistling through clear cracks and holes.
The ramshackle structure sits on four big cinder-
blocks. I swear if he and I pushed very hard on any
of the four sides, the place would collapse.

"Here it is," he says, sheepishly, quietly. "Where
it all began."

This is where Randle lived with his two brothers and single mom—who made $23 a week
working as a maid—until his senior year in high
school, when the family had enough to move to
an actual house.

(I remember writing these two sentences on
my laptop the next day, the first two in the story
on Randle: You can't be proud of a place like this.
You can only be proud of surviving it.)

Randle points to a nail still banged into the

back of the house. "We'd put a bucket of water there, in all kinds of weather. Me and my brothers, one at a time, would stand outside here, and we'd get washed." In the winter, cold high winds would whistle through the place, and the three boys would huddle together, "eight or nine blankets around us and we'd still be cold," he says.

The place looks like an abandoned attic.

We are quiet for a few minutes. I don't know what to say. Randle is embarrassed, and now clearly wishes he hadn't brought me here. This is something worse than poverty.

"Man," he says. "Man! Can't believe it."

I say to him, "Now I know why you play like such a crazy man."

"In my life," he says, "I've chopped cotton, picked watermelons, built fences, worked on an assembly line, worked in an oil field, built scaffolding. You know what? Those jobs are harder than football. So I'll never take it easy in football."

In his career, Randle was a nut job, a guy who did a lot of clownish things. He wasn't a beloved figure. Rather, he was a strange one. But for 36 hours, I walked in his shoes. I saw where he came from. And it was one of the great lessons I ever learned in this job: There's always a reason— good, bad, right or wrong—why a player or coach acts the way he does.

> We are quiet for a few minutes. I don't know what to say. Randle is embarrassed, and now clearly wishes he hadn't brought me here. This is something worse than poverty.

Rod Smart

MEET THE XFL

Las Vegas — February 2001

I am at the first game in the history of the XFL, which—how can I put this now, almost a decade later—you could have sworn from the first second you saw it would crash and burn, because it was so, so strange.

How about a pregame press conference with Vince McMahon, the czar prince of professional wrestling, yelling: "We're gonna show you the snot coming out of a lineman's nose! We're gonna change the way all sports are broadcast!"

How about a cheerleader interviewing a quarterback—during the game—and asking, suggestively: "Do you really know how to score?"

How about a camera in the cheerleaders' dressing room before the game, and the opening possession of the game decided not by coin flip but by two men crashing into each other at midfield, fighting for the ball, and the players being able to have whatever they wanted printed on the backs of their jerseys?

How about covering a sports event and staying three nights at the Hard Rock Hotel, not your local Marriott? (Oooops. Forgot. Who cares what hotel I stay in, other than me?)

All telecast live on NBC. As Dick Ebersol said, when asked before the game why he would ever get involved in this weirdness, "You know what the highest-rated TV show on Saturday night is? Whatever you bring home from Blockbuster."

And so, with this anything-for-ratings backdrop, I look down from the press box at a running back for the Las Vegas Outlaws, in this inaugural game against the New York Hitmen (Outlaws? Hitmen? What? No Connecticut Contract Killers?), ripping off a 46-yard catch and run in the Las Vegas rout. "What is that on his back?" I ask my SI mate in the press box, Leigh Montville. "Is that DEBATE ME? I can't read it."

Binoculars, please.

"It says, HE HATE ME! What the heck is that?"

Everyone is talking about it up in the press box. We're all theorizing what it could possibly mean. But the only one who can tell me for sure is Mr. He Hate Me. So after the final gun, I seek out the player, Rod Smart, a little guy from Western Kentucky trying to scratch and claw his way into pro football.

"Why do you have HE HATE ME on your back?" I wonder.

"You know," he says, "you go out and you're so good, and you hurt your opponent, and it's like, 'They hate me.' So, HE HATE ME."

You know, I didn't major in hieroglyphics in college, nor did I stay at a Holiday Inn Express

Never, ever have I seen a sports venture fall so far so fast. Within three months the XFL was dead. But for a couple of months it was an interesting diversion.

last night. So I'm going to leave that one to you to figure out.

That first game in league history got a 10.3 rating, about equal to a good out-of-market NFL game on a Sunday afternoon. Gigantic. Stunning. So incredible that our little magazine put the league on the cover after its first weekend of football.

Never, ever have I seen a sports venture fall so far so fast. Within three months the XFL was dead. NBC bailed after the first season; the ratings went in the tank once fans got their fill of the wackiness they saw three or four times on TV. Without TV, the league would never last. But for a couple of months it was an interesting diversion.

FEEL-GOOD GUY

Carlisle, Pa. — July 2002

I am standing outside Massey's Frozen Custard stand on Pennsylvania 11 in Carlisle, the main drag in town. I've just beaten the heat after the afternoon practice at Redskins training camp by getting a vanilla custard cone when I see cornerback Darrell Green riding down the busy thoroughfare on his 10-speed bike. Before I can yell hello to him, I see that a car has stopped, and two kids have gotten out, and they've waved for Green to stop. He stops. He rubs one of the little boys' heads. He signs autographs for both kids.

Darrell Green

Green has both feet on the ground, and he is straddling his bike. I'm sure he wants to hop back on it, but now there's a scene, and he stands there for a good 10 to 15 minutes, signing every last autograph and posing for pictures with fans.

And then he's off, back to the dorm for dinner and meetings. And all I can think is: Why doesn't every team practice out in the world somewhere, with players and coaches available in public, mingling with the people who make them so rich? It's the least they can do. It's the least the owners can do. But when I raise this point, I hear things like, "We can control our costs better if we stay at our home facility." Or, "We don't like to break up our routine, and we don't like to take the time it takes to move." Or, "Taking players away is so yesterday. Players are together enough now, bonding and building chemistry. We don't need to bond at some small-college dorm in the middle of Pennsylvania."

No, you don't. You don't have to do any of that. But I can tell you this: There are 40 people somewhere in the U.S. today who either love Darrell Green or love the Washington Redskins just a little bit more because Darrell Green stopped and made their day on that hot afternoon in Carlisle. And there aren't enough times in sports today when feel-good moments happen. There should be more. Many more.

> Why doesn't every team practice out in the world somewhere, with players and coaches available in public, mingling with the people who make them so rich? It's the least they can do.

Dan Marino

DAN THE MAN

New York City — February 2003

I am in a bar on the Lower East Side of Manhattan for the wrap party of the HBO *Inside the NFL* season. Much wine is being drunk, and the occasion is festive, for many reasons. One is that we feel we have a legitimate shot at the first-ever sports Emmy for Best Studio Sports Show, something the powers at HBO feel slighted about because the show, despite a great run, has never won. (Indeed, we did win, and in fact we won three Emmys in a four-year span for Best Studio Sports Show.) Another reason: We had a bunch of oenophiles on the show.

But I have to leave early. My mother is quite ill up in Connecticut (she would die eight weeks later) and I'd neglected her far too often during the crush of the football season. (You know how people say of überbusy kids who might give dying or deceased parents short shrift, "Oh, Dad would have wanted you to work," or, "Mom would have wanted you to take care of your family?" That was my mother, to a T. She loved me being around, but she loved more the fact that I was happily married, with two great kids and doing a job I loved—and, in turn, she loved me having.) Anyway, it was time for me to cut off the wining at two glasses and head up to Hartford to see her in the hospital.

I say a few quiet goodbyes to the crew and friends on the show. The place is noisy and mobbed—maybe 200 people with the show and bar patrons clogging the floor—and so I'm not going to get to say a personal so-long to the 50 or 60 folks that I should. And all the way in the back, sitting at a table, is Dan Marino, with a glass of Pinot, I think, in his hands.

Marino had been friendly to me all season. Not anything like best-friend friendly, but very much a team player and always willing to help me or take my advice on what he might say regarding whatever the news of the week was. When I covered Marino as a player, I found him to be accommodating, but extremely cautious with anything he ever said to me. Never did I feel he was leveling with me, but I don't think I was alone.

And so now, on my way out the door, I wave to get his attention, from maybe 50 feet away, just to say goodbye, and I give him a quick salute and mouth, "Thank you." He holds up a finger. Then he makes his way through the crowd. It takes a couple of minutes. And I tell him he didn't have to do that, and I hold out my hand to shake and say something like, "It's been great working with you this year."

But he doesn't take my hand. He hugs me. He knows my mom is not well. And he says in my

There's nothing he could do, of course. But it's a story I tell to anyone who asks me about Dan Marino, because it's the real him. A person. A good person.

ear, "Buddy, if there's anything I can do, anything at all, you've got my number. Just call me. Whatever I can do, I'll do."

There's nothing he could do, of course. But it's a story I tell to anyone who asks me about Dan Marino, because it's the real him. A person. A good person.

ENDGAME

Englewood, Colo. — August 2005

I am in the Broncos' practice bubble. A wicked rainstorm is pelting the area, forcing the team to hold its afternoon training-camp practice inside in a combo indoor-soccer/football facility a few hundred yards from the team's outdoor fields.

I am watching Jerry Rice's attempt to make the Broncos, two months shy of his 43rd birthday. I keep hearing, "Rice should retire," and "Rice is embarrassing himself," and "Rice is tarnishing his legacy" in the media and in the public. And I hate it. Just hate it. Who are we to tell a player when to retire? Why can't a player play until they rip the uniform off him? Don't we want to see that kind of love of the game from our heroes? And that's all we've heard from Rice. In one form or another, what he's been saying since getting to training camp is, *I want to see if I can make this team and still contribute, because I love playing*

Jerry Rice

football. That attitude is why we love this player. It makes Rice Rice.

So I have come to see if he can do it. On this particular play, he is being covered by free-agent rookie cornerback Brandon Browner of Oregon State. A couple of days earlier, Browner had his 21st birthday; he was nine months old when Rice was drafted by the San Francisco 49ers. Here's an interesting matchup: the man most people consider the best wide receiver of all time (I don't, but let's not quibble over that) against a player who is a long shot to play a single game in the NFL. (As it turns out, Brandon Browner never does.)

Rice lines up wide-right. He tugs on his gloves, flexing his hands, and assumes that classic Rician stance, leaning forward, glancing over at the line of scrimmage so he gets a perfect jump as soon as the ball is snapped. Browner gives him room, five or six yards. Jake Plummer takes the snap, drops back five steps, and surveys the field. Rice sprints hard down the right side. Speed has never been his forte, but if he's going to make this team as the third (doubtful) or fourth (possible) receiver, he's going to have to be able to beat Brandon Browner in man coverage down the right sideline.

Rice sprints. Browner sprints. They are stride for stride, for 15 yards. Rice can't get an inch on the kid. Plummer throws elsewhere.

When Rice is standing on the steps in Canton for his Pro Football Hall of Fame induction a year from now, I'm not going to be thinking anything about a tarnished legacy. I'll be thinking of a man who tried to play the game he loved for as long as he could.

I watch a couple more plays, Rice on kids, and he makes a play, then is blanketed on a couple more. I suppose I should think: *How sad. Jerry Rice doesn't know when to say when. It's pathetic. Someone's got to tell him to quit.* But I don't. I'm glad he's trying. It's noble.

Within a month, Rice retires. He knows he's not going to make the Broncos, and it's time for him to recognize that his skills have eroded to the point that he has to give up. But my last memory of Rice the player will be watching him sprint hard to try to beat a kid who was in diapers when he broke into the league. And when Rice is standing on the steps in Canton for his Pro Football Hall of Fame induction a year from now, I'm not going to be thinking anything about a tarnished legacy. I'll be thinking of a man who tried to play the game he loved for as long as he could.

THE MAVERICK

San Antonio — October 2005

I am standing with Michael Vick in the visitors' locker room at the Alamodome after a game between Atlanta and New Orleans. (Remember when the Saints lost their 2005 home season due to Hurricane Katrina, and moved here?) He is installing a diamond earring when we begin to speak. (I've always considered it sort of funny to

Michael Vick

interview a man while he's putting on earrings.) He is happy. It has been a good day.

Vick is not one of those body-of-work, classic NFL quarterbacks. He will complete 48% of his throws one week and bring his offense to a grinding halt more than a few times a game. But there are times when Vick's brilliance is so tempting, so tantalizing, that you think he can work as a long-term winning quarterback. One of those times happened today, about 45 minutes earlier, out there on the field.

The score was 31–31, with 14 seconds left in the fourth quarter. The ball rested at the Saints' 32-yard line. Atlanta ball, third-and-three. The Falcons wanted to get a few yards closer to field goal range, preferably with the ball in the center of the field, and then they'd use their last timeout to stop the clock, kick the field goal and walk off with a win. So through Vick's helmet speaker, offensive coordinator Greg Knapp called for a Warrick Dunn run up the gut, a safe play designed to gain a yard or two and leave the ball between the hashes.

And Vick thought: maybe.

"I couldn't run that play," Vick says, twirling in the earring. "Saints had a 'zero' blitz on. Everyone's coming. The safeties were down, corners down, everyone crowding the line. I hand it off, and we've got a blowup play. They'd kill Warrick."

> There are times when Vick's brilliance is so tempting, so tantalizing, that you think he can work as a long-term winning quarterback.

Vick took the snap, faked a handoff to the grasping and stunned Dunn, put the ball on his left hip, and sprinted around left end for a four-yard gain. First down. Nine seconds left. Two five-yard penalties by the Saints followed, and Todd Peterson's 36-yard field goal at the gun won it.

"You go into a game, a game we really needed, and you do what you have to do to win," Vick says. "It's all I know. I've been playing that way since I was at Virginia Tech and before, since I was a kid in the backyard. That's me."

As I write this, it's the summer of 2010. Michael Vick, 30, has finished his 20-month jail sentence stemming from dogfighting convictions and is heading into his second year as a backup in Philly. He is driven to be a starter somewhere. The only way he can return to a starting role is by showing that he's accurate enough over a long stretch, and I don't see that happening this year, stuck behind Kevin Kolb. But if Jake Delhomme gets another shot at $7 million a year as he's doing with Cleveland this season, Vick's day will come again too.

HURRICANE RELIEF
New Orleans — April 2006

I am in Musicians' Village, the Habitat for Humanity site where homes in the Lower Ninth Ward of the Katrina-ravaged city are being rebuilt. Two days

Sean Payton

before the NFL draft, my wife and I are wheeling wheelbarrows, carrying bricks, digging trenches for basements; you name it, we're the mules. In town to cover the Saints' first draft with Sean Payton as coach, I figure the football world can get along without me for seven blue-collar hours.

And today I am lucky. Very lucky. My friend Jack Bowers works for Habitat, and I mentioned to him that I would ask Payton and the Saints' G.M., Mickey Loomis, both very good guys, to stop by during lunchtime today in a break from their final draft prep. I didn't push it at all, but I told them that it'd be great for morale if they could come over to the site and shake some hands and talk to the volunteers. Payton said sure, they'd come by.

So it's maybe 10:30 in the morning, and all of sudden we see six or eight black Suburbans with tinted windows buzz into the neighborhood. This morning Jack had said that President Bush was in town and might be coming today. And so here comes the advance team, and we've all got to leave the site for a few minutes and go through an X-ray machine before we can go back to work. And then I hear the neighborhood has been sealed off within two or three blocks in all directions. Uh-oh. How's the coach going to get in? He's not, a Secret Service guy tells me; nobody gets in now. So I go to the guy who looks like the

I told Payton and Loomis that it'd be great for morale if they could come over to the site and shake some hands and talk to the volunteers. Payton said sure, they'd come by.

boss of the advance team, tell him the story, and phone calls are made, and walkie-talkies are activated, and bing-bang-boom, Payton and Loomis are told to be at a specific location at noon, and they get there, and they're hustled through about 10 minutes after the President arrives.

"How cool is this?" Payton says when he walks in the place and sees the President. Payton's a Republican, so this is one heck of a lot better than a chicken-salad sandwich on white bread back at the office while studying that seventh-round cornerback he might draft.

From behind, before he sees, Payton gets a clap on the back from the President of the United States. "How about this!" Bush calls out to his partners on the site, mayor Ray Nagin and governor Kathleen Blanco. "A 42-year-old guy from Eastern Illinois, coaching the Saints, living his dream!"

"Only in America!" Nagin says.

"Hey," says the biggest University of Texas football fan in the District of Columbia. "Who's gonna take Vince Young Saturday?"

"Wish I knew, sir," says Payton.

They chat for a few minutes. Football, mostly. And then both have to move on. Payton's thrilled to have met the President. Now he'd be more thrilled if his day goes as well on Saturday.

"How cool is this?" Payton says when he walks in the place and sees the President.

"Maybe," he says, "we can meet the other Bush on Saturday."

Reggie, that is.

JOE COLLEGE

Madison, Wis. — April 2007

Joe Thomas

I am on the fringe of campus at the University of Wisconsin. Never been here before, even though it came down to Wisconsin or Ohio University as my college choice—you know, back in the days when kids didn't visit 24 schools in order to actually make a college choice—before picking OU. I arrive at the home of a man about to be very rich and find a man who might be the most normal Joe College kid in the United States.

"Welcome to our humble abode," says a smiling and hulking Joe Thomas, the best offensive lineman in America.

The place, I'd guess, is two neglected years from being condemned, but I love it. The art on the wall in the living room—where, by the way, there is a hole in the floor, with the basement in full view—is a framed poster of John Belushi from *Animal House*. You know, the one with Belushi wearing the COLLEGE T-shirt. In the room off the living room, two of Thomas's teammates are sleeping, while another, defensive back Ben Strickland, is watching *Pardon the Interruption* on the TV. The best part of the room, easy, is the six-point trophy buck mounted on the wall with a padded red bra hanging from the highest point. "I was just doing laundry one day, and it snuck its way into my clothes," Strickland says mischievously. In the kitchen, right next to the sink, is a Miller Lite tap. Active.

We walk upstairs. I think there's a floor in Thomas's room, but I can't swear to it. Never saw it. On his desk sits his laptop, which rests on four legs of toilet paper.

> Thomas tells me he won't be going to New York for the NFL draft a couple of weeks down the road. "Going fishing with my dad," he says. "Some of my best memories are fishing with my dad, and I want to make sure I do that as often as I can before my life changes for good."

Thomas tells me he won't be going to New York for the NFL draft a couple of weeks down the road. "Going fishing with my dad," he says. "Some of my best memories are fishing with my dad, and I want to make sure I do that as often as I can before my life changes for good."

I ask him what he's going to do with the millions he'll make from his rookie contract.

He thinks for a few seconds. "Probably put most of it away. Invest it. But there is one thing I really want."

Finally! Now we'll get to the Bentley, or the house in the Bahamas, or the mansion for his parents outside Milwaukee.

"I'd love to have a little hunting cabin me and my friends could use in the off-season, way out in the woods," he says. "That's all I really want, other than the normal stuff you need to live."

I never root for players. At least I'm not supposed to. But after having a bratwurst and some cheeses curds with Thomas and his girlfriend that night, I leave Madison thinking: I hope where he plays, Joe Thomas holds his foes sackless.

Postscript: Depending on whom you believe, Thomas allowed either one or two sacks in his 16-game rookie season. Good guys *can* finish first.

HE'S THE MANNING

Terre Haute, Ind. — July 2007

I am in a storage shed next to the field at Rose-Hulman Institute, site of Indianapolis Colts training camp, where I'm about to interview Peyton Manning after a broiler of a practice. The shed houses the big lawn mowers, field liners and all that stuff used to take care of fields. There are two folding chairs set up. The Colts' p.r. man, Craig Kelley, has me wait in one. Manning will sit in the other.

Why are we here? Because no one would ever think Peyton Manning would sit in this hot box to do an interview—thus, he'll have the peace and quiet he'd like to have for it.

First, a word about what I've just seen at the morning practice. Two things: Manning was out early, working with two camp quarterbacks who

Peyton Manning

had little chance of making even the practice squad. He's out there teaching these kids, including Temple's Mike McGann, the intricacies of the five-step drop, done right. Then, when they go up against the defense in passing drills, first unit offense against first unit defense, I see Manning throw again and again to rookie first-round pick Anthony Gonzalez. And he keeps audibling, causing Gonzalez and rookie left tackle Tony Ugoh to spend extra time looking back at Manning to make sure they've got the play right. "If I'm going to have confidence in Gonzalez during the season, and I plan to, I need to put him in every position he's going to be in when it counts," Manning says. "And I need Ugoh to make the adjustments he's going to have to make during the game."

And you wonder why the guy has had a little success in the National Football League.

Now Manning is here, and he sits down, dripping with sweat, and I'm going to interview him for SI's NFL Preview Issue. One of my first questions is about what he did for fun in the off-season after winning the Super Bowl. I've always enjoyed his mastery of detail. He's anal, with a capital *A*.

This is what he says. "I'm just a football meat-head. I did *Saturday Night Live* this year just to have fun. I'm a lot more nervous for a game. But

> "If I'm going to have confidence in Gonzalez during the season, and I plan to, I need to put him in every position he's going to be in when it counts," Manning says.

preparing for *SNL* was like preparing for a football game. I told them I wanted it to be funny. I went up there on a Monday. It's the same as a football week: Monday and Tuesday you put the plan in; Wednesday, Thursday and Friday you practice, although you only do each script the one time. The nervous thing is on Wednesday. You sit around with the whole crew, cast, cameras and makeup. They give you a stack of scripts and about 30 minutes to read all 40 of them on your own. Then Lorne Michaels reads the scene, and you have to do the reading. There's nothing about character or whatever, and you sound like a moron in front of these people. That's when they decide what's funny and what's not.

"You know what I'd really like to do? I'd like to do one of those reality-TV shows on the ultimate debate—what is the toughest job in sports? You'd put a pitcher in there, a golfer, a basketball player, a tennis player, a hockey player, a football player. I wouldn't have to be the football representative. I'd probably put Brett Favre in there, but I'd write his material. And I would say you can't compare anything to quarterback. A pitcher has no time factor, no hurry. He doesn't like the call from the catcher, he steps off, doesn't waste a timeout. I haven't found one job that really compares to what the quarterback has to go through.

> I'm not trying to keep him. But with Manning, you just can't stop. He has to know what you know.

You take all those things: time, weather, noise and then you get to dealing with the rush, dealing with the speed. And you truly have the game in your hands."

In 51 minutes I got eight questions in. That's how it is when you're with Manning. You end up asking, conversing, conversing, asking, commenting.

Oh, and then he channels his inner Chris Mortensen. "Where've you been so far?" he says.

"Bills, Steelers, Browns, Bengals," I say.

"How's Carson look? What's he doing in practice?"

The p.r. guy's giving me the eye, like, "Let's go! He's got to go!"

I'm not trying to keep him. But with Manning, you just can't stop. He has to know what you know.

SOLITARY MAN

Latrobe, Pa. — July 2007

I am walking from the dining hall at Pittsburgh Steelers training camp at St. Vincent's College, on a road through campus above the sunken football fields. It is early evening. A beautiful, warm, cloudless, humid evening, quiet except for the *whoooosh-whoooosh-whoooosh-whoooosh* of the sprinklers irrigating the green fields. In the distance, the Laurel Highlands glimmer through the

Joe Greene

haze. If anything in the United Stated looked like the meadows of central England, it is where I am standing right now.

To call it bucolic would be an insult to the school.

There is a solitary man about 200 yards ahead of me, on a bench, watching the sprinklers. As I get closer, I can see, and smell, his cigar. It is Joe Greene. Now a scout with the Steelers, he is in camp to look at the new draftees and free agents, evaluating them so the scouts, when they meet in the evening, can throw in their two cents' worth about where the kids might fit, or if they will fit, on the 53-man roster or practice squad.

How about this for a perfect training-camp picture: One of the alltime NFL greats, in the middle of a postcard, in solitude, with cigar smoke twirling above his head, thinking about whatever it is that Joe Greene thinks about when he's alone.

I consider walking up to him, making small talk about the day or the practices or the team or his life or the Steel Curtain or what a beautiful setting this is. Then I thought: Why spoil it? If Greene wanted to talk to people, he'd be inside with the rest of the scouts or the players or the coaches or whoever. There's nothing he can say, or that I could ask, that would make this moment better. Instead, I just stand there, 50 yards away, watching

How about this for a perfect training-camp picture: One of the alltime NFL greats, in the middle of a postcard, in solitude, with cigar smoke twirling above his head, thinking about whatever it is that Joe Greene thinks about when he's alone.

him and soaking in the scene, and then move on.

That's it. Just another reason why training camp is my favorite time of the year.

Mike Tannenbaum

O TANNENBAUM

Kannapolis, N.C. — August 2008

I am in Fieldcrest Cannon Stadium in Kannapolis, about 40 minutes outside of Charlotte. Tomorrow I'm covering Panthers training camp. Tonight I'm with 178 of my closest friends, and a few crickets, watching South Atlantic League baseball. One of the joys of the job is training camp, and a couple of times a summer, relaxing with a few beers and crickets at a minor league game with the stands as empty as possible. I love it.

Bottom of the second. Strange coincidence: I'm on my second Coors Light. The phone rings. I look down and see it's Mike Tannenbaum, the New York Jets' general manager. We'd been talking over the past few days about Brett Favre, and the Jets really, really want Favre to be their quarterback now that he's openly discussing coming out of retirement to play somewhere in 2008. Now that the story's behind us, and Favre and the Jets had their one year together, I can say a few things about how the whole thing unfolded.

"Favre call you yet?" I say.

"No," he said. "Haven't heard from him."

And if something's going to happen, Tannenbaum says, it's got to happen now. It's just getting too late for a quarterback to learn the offense well enough to start opening day for a playoff contender.

Against my better judgment, because I don't give out anyone's cellphone number without permission, I give Tannenbaum Favre's number, and I tell him, "Text him. Don't call. He'll never pick up if he doesn't know the number." Tannenbaum's dying to make the Jets' case to Favre. And then I text Favre, telling him I gave Tannenbaum his number, and if he wants to talk to him, it's up to him. If he doesn't, don't answer the text and don't pick up the phone.

This is a Tuesday night, Aug. 5. That night, Tannenbaum and Favre talk quite late. Then Tannenbaum flies to southern Mississippi the next morning, meets Favre, and he makes a deal with the Packers on a trade for Favre, and flies back with Favre to New Jersey, and tours Favre around the area via helicopter, and then flies with Favre to Cleveland, where the Jets are playing a preseason game on Thursday night, Aug. 7.

Forty-six hours after Tannenbaum gets Favre's cellphone number, Favre walks into Cleveland Browns Stadium to join his new team.

"Pretty crazy couple of days," says Favre. Really?

Forty-six hours after Tannenbaum gets Favre's cellphone number, Favre walks into Cleveland Browns Stadium to join his new team. "Pretty crazy couple of days," he says. Really?

Acknowledgments

I OWE SO MUCH to three managing editors in my 20 years at SPORTS ILLUSTRATED. Mark Mulvoy hired me and taught me a lot about what makes good magazine writing. Even though he didn't have anything to do with the creation of my online column, he's the kind of smart reader who has grown to love the immediacy and opinion that it offers. Bill Colson had the foresight to allow me to take magazine time to work on the column when no one knew what a website was. And my current boss, Terry McDonell, has a keen understanding of the changing media industry and has embraced the column and my Web work the way a modern editor should.

I want to thank the editors of the column over the years. Steve Robinson is the boss who had either the brains or the misfortune to invent Monday Morning Quarterback. He thought people wanted to know what a sportswriter's life was like, and so I have tried to tell people what mine is like. Stefanie Kaufman (née Krasnow) is the finest, most caring and most underrated word person I've met in my years as a writer, and I appreciate how often she saved me from myself over the years. Andrew Perloff trusted me to have good ideas and always had a knack of telling me about the stupid ones without making me feel like a fool. Bobby Clay, the tireless one, caught a record number of stupid mistakes at 3:47 a.m. and kept me honest. Dom Bonvissuto might look 19, but he's got the brains of someone who's, oh, 23. No. Dom's smart, just pushy enough, and a good idea man for a business that changes every 20 minutes or so.

Thanks to Jerry Klein for being there at the beginning, to Mike Silver for ideas when I had none, to Paul Zimmerman for teaching me football, to Tim Layden for a trustworthy ear and to Don Banks for being my sounding board for the last few years (and to tell me when I've really gone off the deep end, which happens about every four days). Thanks to Mark Godich, Mike Bevans and Mark Mravic, SI football editors who have had to grit their teeth while waiting for my magazine copy over the years because of MMQB.

Thanks especially to book editor Larry Burke, who reset the deadline 614 times in the past eight months because I couldn't meet the previous 613. Larry didn't have a life for the past half-year while putting up with mine. Without Larry and Stefanie, this book wouldn't have happened.

Thanks to Starbucks, the Montclair (N.J.) High field hockey and softball programs, airlines, bad hotels, gouging health clubs, Amtrak and annoying cellphone users.

Thanks to the players, coaches, general managers and p.r. people of the NFL for making time for me and MMQB on Sunday nights, and for putting off their own lives for a few minutes to help me do my job. A 1:47 a.m. call from then-Cleveland offensive coordinator Rob Chudzinski comes to mind. Without their help, there would be no MMQB.

And thanks to millions of you, for caring immensely about pro football and, apparently, for caring about the opinions of the luckiest person in sports media history.

Football America photo credits: E. BAKKE/WIREIMAGE.COM (Rice), JOHN BIEVER (Johnson), ALAN DIAZ/AP (Marino), RIC FELD/AP (Vick), MORRY GASH/AP (Favre), JOE GIZA/REUTERS (Green), LEON HALIP/US PRESSWIRE (Greene), MARK E. JOHNSON/AP (Bledsoe), LARRY LAMBRECHT/WIREIMAGE.COM (Madden), PETER READ MILLER (Gogan), JOHN W. MCDONOUGH (Young), AL MESSERSCHMIDT/WIREIMAGE.COM (Davis, Reich, Rozelle), NFL/WIREIMAGE.COM (Randle), AL PEREIRA/GETTY IMAGES (Tannenbaum), BOB ROSATO (Payton), DAMIAN STROHMEYER (Thomas), AL TIELEMANS (Manning), TODD WARSHAW/GETTY IMAGES (Smart)